Teaching the FE Curriculum

Other Titles in the Essential FE Toolkit Series

Books for Lecturers

Teaching the FE Curriculum – Mark Weyers

e-Learning in FE – John Whalley, Theresa Welch and Lee Williamson

FE Lecturer's Survival Guide – Angela Steward

FE Lecturer s Guide to Diversity and Inclusion – Anne-Marie Wright, Sue Colquhoun, Sina Abdi-Jama, Jane Speare and Tracey Partridge.

How to Manage Stress in FE – Elizabeth Hartney

Guide to Teaching 14–19 – James Ogunleye

Ultimate FE Lecturer's Guide – Ros Clos and Trevor Dawn

A to Z of Teaching in FE – Angela Steward

Getting the Buggers Motivated in FE – Sue Wallace

Books for Managers

Everything you need to know about FE policy – Yvonne Hillier

Middle Management in FE – Ann Briggs

Managing Higher Education in Colleges – Gareth Parry, Anne Thompson and Penny Blackie

Survival Guide for College Managers and Leaders – David Collins

Guide to Leadership and Governance in FE – Adrian Perry

Guide to Financial Management in FE – Julian Gravatt

Guide to Race Equality in FE – Beulah Ainley

Ultimate FE Leadership and Management Handbook – Jill Jameson and Ian McNay

A to Z for every Manager in FE – Susan Wallace and Jonathan Gravells

Guide to VET – Chris Winch and Terry Hyland

Continuum International Publishing Group
The Tower Building   80 Maiden Lane, Suite 704
11 York Road   New York
SE1 7NX   NY 10038

www.continuumbooks.com

British Library Cataloguing-in-Publication Data
A catalogue record for this book is available from the British Library.

ISBN: 0–8264–8804–8 (paperback)

Library of Congress Cataloging-in-Publication Data
A catalog record for this book is available from the Library of Congress.

Typeset by YHT Ltd, London
Printed and bound in Great Britain by Ashford Colour Press, Gosport, Hampshire

Teaching the FE Curriculum

Encouraging Active Learning in the Classroom

Mark Weyers

continuum

Contents

About this book

As Coffield *et al.* (2004) point out, all teacher–student inter-actions in post–16 learning are embedded in structures of power and regulatory control. Often teachers have limited freedom to choose the strategies they wish to adopt. This book will make practical suggestions, grounded in educational research, for FE teachers trying to meet the institutional demands of a standar-dized curriculum and examination system.

There are many concepts and pedagogical strategies that have developed over the last few decades based on fly-by-night theories laden with the latest edu-jargon. This book will attempt to outline current theory and best practice that is founded in sound empirical research. The majority of the research that underpins this book falls within the realm of what has come to be called *student learning research* (Biggs 1999). This book will demonstrate how some of the research and peda-gogical principles, drawn on concepts originally developed for higher education, which I have found to exist in further edu-cation (Weyers 2005). In addition, while the majority of the practical examples I have given are drawn from my experience teaching Computing and ICT, the general principles can as easily be applied to other subject areas.

The book will present the research in an easily accessible way that leaves educators with the flexibility to personalize their own innovations and adapt these concepts and ideas to their own classrooms and institutions. Additionally, recognizing that teachers do not have the time or the energy to continually reinvent innovative classrooms, this book also provides practical suggestions, based on sound pedagogical principles and strate-gies, to support teachers in transforming teaching and learning in their classrooms.

Series foreword

THE ESSENTIAL FE TOOLKIT SERIES

Jill Jameson
Series Editor

In the autumn of 1974, a young woman newly arrived from Africa landed in Devon to embark on a new life in England. Having travelled half-way round the world, she still longed for sunny Zimbabwe. Not sure what career to follow, she took a part-time job teaching EFL to Finnish students. Having enjoyed this, she studied thereafter for a PGCE at the University of Nottingham in Ted Wragg's Education Department. After teaching in secondary schools, she returned to university in Cambridge, and, after graduating, took a job in ILEA in 1984 in adult education. She loved it: there was something about adult education that woke her up, made her feel fully alive, newly aware of all the lifelong learning journeys being followed by so many students and staff around her. The adult community centre she worked in was a joyful place for diverse multi-ethnic communities. Everyone was cared for, including 90-year-olds in wheelchairs, toddlers in the crèche, ESOL refugees, city accountants in business suits and university level graphic design students. In her eyes, the centre was an educational ideal, a remarkable place in which, gradually, everyone was helped to learn to be who they wanted to be. This was the Chequer Centre, Finsbury, EC1, the 'red house', as her daughter saw it, toddling in from the crèche. And so began the story of a long interest in further education that was to last for many years . . . why, if they did such good work for so many, were FE centres so under-funded and unrecognized, so under-appreciated?

It is with delight that, 32 years after the above story began, I write the Foreword to *The Essential FE Toolkit*, Continuum's new series of 24 books on further education (FE) for teachers and college leaders. The idea behind the *Toolkit* is to provide a comprehensive guide to FE in a series of compact, readable books. The suite of 24 individual books are gathered together to provide the practitioner with an overall FE toolkit in specialist, fact-filled volumes designed to be easily accessible, written by experts with significant knowledge and experience in their individual fields. All of the authors have in-depth understanding of further education. But 'Why is further education important? Why does it merit a whole series to be written about it?' you may ask.

At the Association of Colleges Annual Conference in 2005, in a humorous speech to college principals, John Brennan said that, whereas in 1995 further education was a 'political backwater', by 2005 it had become 'mainstream'. John recalled that since 1995 there had been '36 separate Government or Government-sponsored reports or white papers specifically devoted to the post–16 sector'. In our recent regional research report (2006) for the Learning and Skills Development Agency, my co-author Yvonne Hillier and I noted that it was no longer 'raining policy' in FE, as we had described earlier (Hillier and Jameson, 2003): there is now a torrent of new initiatives. We thought, in 2003, that an umbrella would suffice to protect you. We'd now recommend buying a boat to navigate these choppy waters, as it looks as if John Brennan's 'mainstream' FE, combined with a tidal wave of government policies will soon lead to a flood of new interest in the sector, rather than end anytime soon.

There are good reasons for all this government attention on further education. In 2004/05, student numbers in LSC council-funded further education increased to £4.2 million, total college income was around £6.1 billion, and the average college had an annual turnover of £15 million. Further education has rapidly increased in national significance regarding the need for ever greater achievements in UK education and skills training for millions of learners, providing qualifications and workforce training to feed a UK national economy hungrily in competition with other OECD nations. The 120 recommendations of the Foster Review (2005) therefore in the main encourage colleges to focus their work on vocational skills, social inclusion and achieving academic progress. This series is here to consider all three of these areas and more.

The series is written for teaching practitioners, leaders and managers in the 572 FE/LSC-funded institutions in the UK, including FE colleges, adult education and sixth form institutions, prison education departments, training and workforce development units, local education authorities and community agencies. The series is also written for PGCE/Cert Ed/City & Guilds Initial and continuing professional development (CPD) teacher trainees in universities in the UK, USA, Canada, Australia, New Zealand and beyond. It will also be of interest to staff in the 600 Jobcentre Plus providers in the UK and to many private training organisations. All may find this series of use and interest in learning about FE educational practice in the 24 different areas of these specialist books from experts in the field.

Our use of this somewhat fuzzy term 'practitioners' includes staff in the FE/LSC-funded sector who engage in professional practice in governance, leadership, management, teaching, training, financial and administration services, student support services, ICT and MIS technical support, librarianship, learning resources, marketing, research and development, nursery and crèche services, community and business support, transport and estates management. It is also intended to include staff in a host of other FE services including work-related training, catering, outreach and specialist health, diagnostic additional learning support, pastoral and religious support for students. Updating staff in professional practice is critically important at a time of such continuing radical policy-driven change, and we are pleased to contribute to this nationally and internationally.

We are also privileged to have an exceptional range of authors writing for the series. Many of our series authors are renowned for their work in further education, having worked in the sector for thirty years or more. Some have received OBE or CBE honours, professorships, fellowships and awards for contributions they have made to further education. All have demonstrated a commitment to FE that makes their books come alive with a kind of wise guidance for the reader. Sometimes this is tinged with world-weariness, sometimes with sympathy, humour or excitement. Sometimes the books are just plain clever or a fascinating read, to guide practitioners of the future who will read these works. Together, the books make up a considerable portfolio of assets for you to take with you through your journeys in further education. We hope the experience of reading the books will be interesting, instructive and pleasurable and that experience gained from them will last, renewed, for many seasons.

It has been wonderful to work with all of the authors and with Continuum's UK Education Publisher, Alexandra Webster, on this series. The exhilarating opportunity of developing such a comprehensive toolkit of books probably comes once in a lifetime, if at all. I am privileged to have had this rare opportunity, and I thank the publishers, authors and other contributors to the series for making these books come to life with their fantastic contributions to FE.

Dr Jill Jameson
Series Editor
March, 2006

Series introduction

THE ESSENTIAL FE TOOLKIT SERIES

Jill Jameson
Series Editor

Teaching the FE Curriculum – Mark Weyers

Do you know the difference between 'deep', 'strategic' and 'surface' approaches to learning? Do you know how to reduce teaching and learning workloads and achieve excellent results at the same time? Do you understand how to apply innovative student-centred teaching methods that genuinely help students learn, so that they love your lessons and want to come back for more? Do you realise why feedback to students is so important, and how you can stimulate deep learning as well as better examination results, by giving effective feedback?

This fascinating book on *Teaching the FE Curriculum* by Dr Mark Weyers will help you to understand a variety of under-pinning concepts about teaching and managing the curriculum in FE in ways that will enable you to try out innovative, effective new teaching methods to encourage both high quality teaching and deep learning in the classroom. If you have ever needed help with lesson preparation, wanted to understand the best ways to teach, or felt you would like to know more about how to become an excellent lecturer in FE, this book is for you.

Mark observes that a heavy workload is linked to a surface approach in learning. He notes also that deep approaches to learning and studying are related to what students perceive as good teaching. Drawing on his own experience as an FE lec-turer, on extensive research in the learning and skills sector and on a range of important prior pedagogical research studies, Mark encourages lecturers to teach in a way that enables stu-dents to adopt a deep learning approach. In this book, lecturers learn how to develop and demonstrate a personal interest in the subject they teach, how to bring out its structure, its in-depth patterns and underlying principles of knowledge in critical ways directly related to real-world experience, to stimulate students. At a time when the Foster Review (2005), the government White Paper on FE (2006) and the Quality Improvement Agency (QIA) are calling for widespread rapid improvements in teaching and learning across the FE sector, this book provides timely, essential reading for FE lecturers. The FE education system is changing to meet the needs of its enhanced role as the major UK skills and education post-16 provider: a renewed focus on excellence in teaching and learning is vital. Don't be left behind in your teaching methods: learn how to change your role as a teacher and facilitator of learning using effective evidence-based methods to ensure that your students are fascinated by your subject area and want to study more.

Mark examines a wide range of different approaches in the classroom, describing learning conversations, instructional strategies, constructivist approaches and problem-based learning activities. He observes that students need to take ownership and responsibility for their learning and that lecturers can facilitate this effectively by stimulating interest in learning activity, using, for example, case studies and Socratic questioning approaches. Written in an iterative, recursive style that slowly builds up, in spiral-like progression, a profoundly important argument relating to the nature of knowledge and of student-centred learning in FE, Mark's book is essential reading for lecturers. I recommend to you this excellent guide to teaching the FE curriculum.

Dr Jill Jameson
Director of Research
School of Education and Training
University of Greenwich
j.jameson@gre.ac.uk

1 Teaching realities

The aim (of education) must be the training of independently acting and thinking individuals who, however, can see in the service to the community their highest life achievement.

Albert Einstein

Introduction

This book, and much of the research I have done to date, has developed from the unease that I felt teaching in the further education (FE) sector. As a teacher of Computing and ICT, I became disillusioned with the confines within which I found myself having to teach. In the midst of masses of paperwork, largely put in place as mechanisms of quality assurance and college bureaucracy, I found that the perscriptive nature of the curriculum and assessment procedures left me little autonomy as a practitioner to provide innovative teaching that I felt encouraged students to engage with the subject.

Further, I found my students were not interested in innovative teaching methods; they wanted to know what questions they could expect to see and exactly what they needed to memorize to get a good grade in their examinations. This was disconcerting, as I knew that it led mainly to didactic methods of teaching often with large portions of class time being spent practising examination questions. I knew my students were not really developing an understanding of the subject area but were studying it to remember it well enough to pass an examination. I began to wonder if there was a way I could provide a balance between the constraints a national curriculum and examination assessment regime imposed on my classroom while still offering innovative teaching methods which encouraged students to learn, enjoy and understand the subject area. This book is my answer to that question and in the following chapters I attempt to explain the theoretical underpinnings of the strategies and techniques that I have used to encourage students to engage at a deeper level with their studies.

The changing face of education

Not surprisingly, the Learning and Skills Council (LSC), the governing body of the FE sector, began to see a need for reform and drafted a discussion document called *Success for All: Reforming further education and training*, which outlined the crucial issues that were degrading the quality of teaching and learning in the FE sector. It argued that funding greatly affects teaching, learning and assessment and that the FE system is permeated by a prevailing audit culture with three-year funding plans linked to minimum acceptable levels of performance, with extra funding for the achievement of 'improvement targets' (see DfES 2002b).

In November 2002, the second version of *Success for All* (DfES 2002b) document set out a strategy for investment and reform. A key element of the strategy was to position teaching and learning as a central concern and establish a standards unit to identify and disseminate best practice and to guide learning and teaching provision (DfES 2002b, p. 5).

Traditionally, vocational courses (e.g. BTEC diploma, GNVQ Foundation, Intermediate and Advanced) were a way of providing students with less than average abilities the necessary training needed for employment, while the General Certificate of Education (GCE) Advanced level is one of the main academic examinations taken by post-compulsory students. Students can obtain an AS qualification and advance into the second year of a course to obtain the full A level qualification. The AS level qualification is composed of three modules while the A2 qualification is composed of a further three modules. One module is a coursework component (which is teacher assessed) and the other two modules are assessed by a final examination.

The Tomlinson Report (Tomlinson 2004a), written by the Working Group on 14–19 Reform, was set up in Spring 2003 to address issues of low post–16 participation and achievement, an over-burdensome curriculum and assessment system and a fragmented system of vocational qualifications. The report argues that there are currently too many qualifications and specifications and the current mix of coursework and formal assessment means that students have too many external exams.

The Tomlinson Report (Tomlinson 2004b, p. 1) answers the question 'why do we need reform?' with the following:

> The choices young people make between age 14 and 19 affect their whole lives. So, the curriculum they study, the examinations they sit and the qualifications they earn are all crucially important.

Further, Elwood (1999) notes, the A level uses traditional assessment methods and a high proportion of the syllabus is examined through final exams in which questions require a high degree of interpretation and specialized vocabulary. In addition, she states, 'the A level remains narrowly focused with achievement being expressed and assessed through written exposition and the recall of procedures and knowledge.' (p. 190)

The influence of examination boards

The design of curriculum, its content and assessment are largely determined by the Qualifications and Curriculum Authority (QCA) and examination awarding bodies. Targets for retention and achievement exert a strong influence on teaching and learning in the classroom. Coffield et al. (2004) argue that the FE system is under a great strain because of the pressure created by the modular structure of qualifications, fragmented teaching teams with 40 per cent of FE teachers on temporary contracts, and limited course hours to cover a packed curriculum.

A review (Harlen and Deakin Crick 2002) by the Evidence for Policy and Practice Information and Co-ordinating Centre (EPPI-Centre) on the impact of summative assessment (year end examinations) on student motivation found that 'high stakes' assessment (i.e. assessment that determines progression) encourages a transmission model of teaching. This suggests that teachers teaching in an environment with a strong focus on standardized testing tend to take a more didactic lecture-style approach to their teaching.

This strong emphasis on examinations has spawned a process-product metaphor of education. As Lumby (2003 p. 3) argues, 'government initiatives in the further education sector have aimed at embedding new ways of thinking about students as customers, communities as markets and leaders as enacting nationally designated standards.' Further, the process of education is built within a framework that will ensure an end product of positive academic achievement (i.e. good grades). Lumby argues that the leadership of educational organizations has become big business, while governments worldwide strive to provide a recipe that will transform our educational leaders into agents that can deliver the required performance. Ritzer (2000) called it 'the "Macdonaldisation" of education', representing our changing views, which are beginning to see education as a product to be bought and sold. As Lumby (p. 4) puts it, 'we have come to accept the necessity for conformity to standard input and output, of treating learners as customers, of using education to primarily serve the needs of the economy, of shouldering the business imperative of remaining financially viable.'

Examination boards fuel this metaphor and have a top-down influence on teaching and learning that directs the academic standards that teachers and colleges must work within in order to meet specific targets considered essential to ensure a quality product is produced within our post-16 institutions. Consequently, examination boards direct not only the assessment methods used for these subjects, but put teachers in a position in which they must adapt their teaching to standardized testing regimes while concurrently feeling the pressure to cover all the subject specifications. This process–product metaphor of education forces us as teachers to focus solely on the 'end-product' (i.e. examination scores) rather than on the process of teaching and learning.

This raises the critical question: "What academic outcomes do we wish our students to have achieved at the completion of their education?" Bransford and his colleagues at Vanderbilt University (CTGV 1991) argue that we must teach students to think effectively, reason, problem-solve and develop learning skills while Perkins (1991) argues the basic goals of education are 'retention, understanding and the active use of knowledge and skills'. Arguably, teaching children to think, critically analyse and problem-solve is a significant aspect of contemporary education. However, the institutional frameworks and the strong focus on examination boards and national curricula that currently exist may have a negative effect on classroom learning. The increasing focus on standardized testing, quality assurance (Ofsted) and attaining qualifications seems to be working against the aims that the system espouses.

Entwistle and Smith (2002) explain that while examination syllabuses and their associated assessment procedures form an initial target, the pressure for public accountability and reliable measures of student achievement (i.e. student grades that accurately reflect learning) lead to 'an overemphasis on factual accuracy and pre-packed descriptive understandings' (p. 337). The researchers use the example of the Scottish biology syllabuses of the Standard Grade (14–16) and Higher (17+), which have an emphasis on predominantly factual knowledge. They point out that, where understanding is specified, no more than the 'descriptive' level seems to be expected and there is little attempt to present the subject as a coherent whole.

As Entwistle and Smith observe, formal syllabuses and the type of examination questions set substantially affect how teachers present the subject to students. In addition, while teachers could encourage students to reach the highest level of understanding, both teacher and student may not see the point of going beyond the expectations of the examination board specifications in light of the many other external influences that make demands on students' lives (i.e. peers, part-time job, family). As Entwistle and Smith argue, examination board specifications can act as a limit to the level of understanding achieved when a limit is put on the level of understanding expected.

The Tomlinson Report (Tomlinson 2004a, p. 4) addresses these issues and argues that less external assessment should allow teachers to bring classes to life through engaging and innovative teaching, as less time would need to be spent preparing pupils for external exams.

In a previous case study (Weyers 2005), I investigated the relationship between staff's and students' perceptions of the teaching–learning environment and their approaches to teaching and studying in a sixth-form college. I found that a link exists between the size of the curriculum, the teaching methods teachers use and the demands made on the student by the course. Teachers tend to keep student-centred learning activities to a minimum when their workload and planning is high and they tend to focus on knowledge transmission (didactic lecture-style methods) at the expense of student understanding. Meeting examination board specifications takes precedence over developing understanding in the classroom.

Further, students feel that examination board assessments are not a measure of understanding but of quantified knowledge (i.e. how much students know and can remember). When the demands made by the course are manageable and when teachers encourage understanding in the classroom students tend to use deep approaches to studying. However, in order to deal with the large amounts of subject information at the end of the academic year, students tend to adopt surface approaches (rote-memorization) for studying and subsequently course satisfaction and final examination grades tend to be lower. Further, student examination grades tend to be higher when students system-atically organize their study time and put effort and con-centration into their studying.

Summary of main points

- Examination board specifications can act as a ceiling to the level of understanding expected of students.
- Teachers tend to keep student-centred learning activities to a minimum when their workload and planning is high and they tend to focus on knowledge transmission (didactic lecture-style methods) at the expense of student understanding.
- Meeting examination board specifications seems to take

precedence over developing understanding in the classroom.

- Students feel that examination board assessments are not a measure of understanding but are a measure of quantified knowledge (i.e. how much students know and can remember).
- When their workload is manageable, students tend to use deep approaches to studying.
- When teachers encourage understanding in the classroom, students tend to use deep approaches to studying.
- To manage substantive subject information at the end of the academic year, students tend to adopt surface approaches (rote memorization) to studying and subsequently course satisfaction and final examination grades tend to be lower.
- Student examination grades tend to be higher when students systematically organize their study time and put effort and concentration into their studying.

Websites of interest

The Association of Colleges (AOC); www.aoc.co.uk
The AOC promotes the interests of further education colleges in England and Wales.
Last accessed: 30 September 2005

The Department of Education and Skills (DfES); www.dfes.co.uk
Last accessed: 15 September 2005

The Learning and Skills Council (LSC); www.lsc.gov.uk
The LSC is responsible for funding and planning education and training for students over 16 years old in England.
Last accessed: 02 October 2005

The Quality Improvement Agency (QIA); www.qia.org.uk
The QIA was created to speed up quality improvement, increase participation and raise standards and achievement. The QIA's role is to create a strong strategic focus on improving quality in the sector.
Last accessed: 10 January 2006

Lifelong Learning UK; www.lluk.org
Lifelong Learning UK (LLUK) is the new sector skills council responsible

for the professional development of all those working in the field of lifelong learning. It will support learning providers in meeting the challenges of the current skills and education agendas.
Last accessed: 10 January 2006

The Office for Standards in Education (OFSTED); www.ofsted.gov.uk
OFSTED is the non-ministerial government department which helps to improve the quality and standards of education and training.
Last accessed: 11 January 2006

The Times Educational Supplement; www.tes.co.uk
Last accessed: 14 November 2005

Training and Development Agency (TDA); www.tda.gov.uk
Last accessed: 05 December 2005

2 Exploring innovative teaching

*Teaching should be such that what is offered is perceived as a
valuable gift and not as a hard duty.*

Albert Einstein

Prosser and Trigwell (1999) found teachers differed in both
their *conceptions of teaching* and their *approaches to teaching* based
on a series of overlapping categories that distinguish a teacher-
focus (linked to information transmission) from a student-focus
(that emphasized conceptual change). Therefore, the approach
adopted by teachers and the ways in which students perceive
them affects the approaches to studying that students adopt,
which subsequently affects the quality of learning achieved.

Conceptions of teaching

In a review of schoolteachers' beliefs and attitudes Calderhead
(1996) found that the ways that teachers interact with their
students depends on their knowledge and understanding of
teaching and learning. Research on teaching identifies three
main forms of knowledge related to teaching – subject matter,
teaching and managing learning, and the relationship with the
learner (Wittrock 1986). Shulman (1987) argues that pedagogical content knowledge – a combination of subject content
and pedagogical knowledge – plays a crucial role in teaching.

Teachers can differ in both their knowledge and underlying
philosophies about teaching, which affects the way in which
they teach (Prosser and Trigwell 1999). At the least sophisti-
cated level, their ideas of teaching focus solely on the transmission of knowledge, while a higher level of understanding
focuses on an understanding of how learning takes place. Biggs

(1989) distinguishes between three separate 'conceptions of teaching' derived from his work in higher education, which can also be easily applied to further education. He describes these conceptions of teaching as quantitative, institutional and qualitative.

Those who take a quantitative view of teaching feel that teaching is the transmission of knowledge from the teacher to the student. From this perspective, a good teacher is one who has a solid grasp of their subject and can communicate that knowledge clearly and effectively. Those who take an institutional view of teaching feel that teaching is the proficient orchestration of teaching skills, and an effective management of the classroom, its teaching and its learning resources. Finally, those who take a qualitative view of teaching feel that teaching is the facilitation of learning and a good teacher supports their students while they construct meaning that is contextual and personally relevant. The learning environment is student-focused and knowledge is built by the student rather than imparted by the teacher (Biggs 1989).

Effective teaching methods

As the education system continues to be redefined to meet the needs of a changing world, alternative methods of teaching continue to be explored and compared to determine the most effective methods for facilitating learning. As the definition of education continues to change in response to societal demands, the role of the teacher changes and new pedagogical theories, teaching methods and instructional strategies are developed. However, while students' characteristics and societal expectations continue to change, traditional methods and modes of instruction are still employed by a large number of teachers. In many classrooms, the principle role of the teacher is to transmit subject information (often in a lecture-style format) to learners. Students attend to the teacher and learn by absorbing this information. Educational theory refers to this form of direct instruction as instructivism (Good and Brophy 1991; Rosenshine and Stevens 1986). Within this framework, the teacher's ability to make effective eye contact and use persuasive questioning techniques while structuring the learning environment into manageable chunks of information is crucial.

Central to the debate over teaching effectiveness is the thrust to use alternative teaching strategies in the classroom. Alternative teaching strategies such as constructivist-based and problem-based strategies are student-centred and focus on students as agents in the construction of their own knowledge rather than as active receptors of information in the classroom. Fundamental to these strategies is the principle that knowledge is not directly transmitted from the teacher to the student but is actively built by the learner. Berryman (1991) argues that students who do not actively participate in the learning process exert limited attention to the task, adopt a passive learning style that models an attitude of 'waiting it out', characterized by a failure to involve themselves in the process of learning. This principle states that students need to be agents in the construction of their own knowledge rather than active receivers of information in the classroom.

The thrust of alternative methods of teaching in the classroom is fuelled by those adverse to the dependence on rote memorization as a pedagogical strategy (Lipman 1991). The view that knowledge is not directly transmitted from the teacher to the student, but is actively built by the learner, underlies the basic premise of constructivist theories. Constructivists argue that 'knowledge is not passively received but built up by the cognizing subject' (von Glasersfeld 1995). Thus, the theory focuses on the process of understanding as opposed to rote memorization (Jennings 1994). Constructivists shift the focus from knowledge as a product to knowing as a process.

Lizzio et al. (2002) found that the type of academic environment within which students are expected to learn (e.g. workload and teaching quality) has an impact on how students approach their learning and studying and the quality of the outcomes they are able to achieve. The teaching methods we use in the classroom affect how our students learn and engage with the subject information. To improve teaching and our students' subsequent learning outcomes, we need to understand the complexities of the teaching–learning environment. Figure 1 depicts the complex process that occurs between the student,

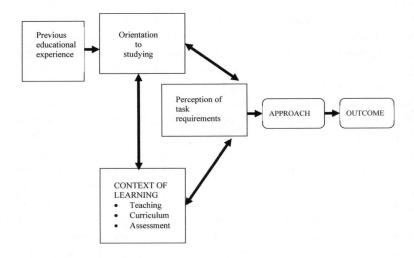

Figure 1 Student learning in context
Source: Ramsden (1992, p. 83)

the teaching–learning environment and students' approaches to learning and studying.

A student-centred versus teacher-centred classroom

Constructivist-based approaches, which are student-centred and emphasize understanding and critical thinking, tend to create learning environments that encourage students to take a deep approach to their studying (covered in Chapter 3). A student using a deep approach attempts to interpret meaning in a variety of ways and make links between new information and their current knowledge and understanding. Conversely, a surface approach, which is often associated with many traditional instructivist-based teaching methods, employs active reproduction strategies (e.g. rote memorization) to remember subject information. A student using a surface approach to studying, which is considered unreflective, concentrates on memorizing the material with limited attention paid to understanding the information (Marton and Säljö 1976, 1997; Thomas and Bain 1984). As teachers, we have seen both approaches in our classrooms. Students who take a surface approach want to know exactly what information to memorize to pass the examination while students who take a deep approach show interest in the subject and try to understand how the information is applicable to the real world.

A similar dichotomy was found by Scardamelia and Bereiter (1987), who noted a distinction between knowledge-telling and knowledge-transforming when students write essays. While 'telling' is considered the passive transfer of information from text to paper, 'transformation' enables the student to actively construct knowledge by relating the subject information in new ways while making novel connections within the subject material. For example, students who hand in essays or coursework that are 'knowledge-telling' will focus on the quantity of information that they can produce and will write down or list everything that they can remember about the topic, while students who are 'knowledge-transforming' will focus on quality rather than quantity and will attempt to develop their own original ideas by making novel links between the topics and subject information.

Good teaching creates learning environments that are process-rich. For us as teachers, this means moving away from teacher-directed classroom situations to embrace more facilitating and collaborative models of teaching and learning. This will allow our students to be self-directing, self-regulating and resourceful learners. Our central role as teachers is not to train students to pass an examination. We need to teach for understanding, not just remembering.

Instructivist teaching methods (or direct instruction) incorporate a teacher-directed curriculum and carefully planned teaching sessions. A central principle of instructivist theory states that teachers make the crucial decisions about the sequence of the learning and subject content (Margules 1996). Teachers base these decisions on their professional training, education and experience. This is the way that most of us learned how to teach and many teacher training programmes centre their teaching of pedagogy on this philosophy.

A lecture-style method of teaching is the primary mode of content delivery. The focus is on the delivery of the subject content itself rather than on the learner or the learning experience. Teachers who take an instructivist approach to their classroom pre-plan a curriculum by breaking down the subject into its component parts and then sequence these topics into an order that ranges from simple to more complex. According to these principles, learning flows largely in a uni-directional path, proceeding from the knowledgeable authority (teacher) to what some refer to as 'the passive learner' (Diaz and Bontenbal 2000). However, proponents of instructivist theory argue that learners take an active, rather than a passive, role in the learning process.

In contrast, in a student-centred classroom, teachers act as facilitators of learning rather than as knowledge experts. However, a common criticism of this approach to learning is that it appears to reduce the curriculum to cater for the whims and interests of the child. Finn and Ratvich (1996) argue that the student-centred principles from which much of modern constructivism originates can appear adverse to the standards and accountability framework within which much of our contemporary education system works.

Teaching methods – a critical distinction

The dichotomy between student-centred and teacher-centred teaching is not necessarily clear-cut. Arguably, instructivist methods of teaching can encourage students to engage on a cognitive level with the subject information by demonstrating new connections within the information and by encouraging students to understand and make sense of newly acquired knowledge by reorganizing it into a form that is personally relevant. Proponents of instructivist methods assert that an essential element of effective instructivist teaching methods is student-teacher interaction. Therefore, it is probable that conceptual change does occur through effective student-teacher interaction. In fact, it would be quite disheartening for us if it did not, considering many of us use this approach quite often in our classrooms.

To solve this debate, it would appear that another category that describes a delivery-method of teaching is needed –

didactic teaching. What differentiates these methods of teaching (student-centred, instructivist, didactic) is the point at which 'knowledge' is created. Didactic teaching is asynchronous, less interactive (i.e. lecture-style methods) and is focused on delivering content. Research into the student experience appears to support the distinction between didactic (content-oriented) and facilitative (learning-oriented) approaches to teaching (Kember 1996). While lessons that are student-centred may more effectively develop adaptive and self-regulating learners (learners who plan their own work) who are better equipped to manage more informal and realistic learning situations (using problem-solving to tackle unfamiliar situations), interactive instructivist-based methods may also prove useful in this regard. Research appears to reinforce the argument that capability derives from congruent processes and independent thinking comes from engaging in independent learning processes (Stephenson and Weil 1992). However, it is probable that traditionally in student learning research (Biggs, 1999) instructivist methods of teaching have been considered synonymous with content-oriented didactic methods of instruction (i.e. lecture style).

'Didactic teaching' methods are teacher-centred, lecture-style chalk-and-talk methods of teaching in which a large majority of the lesson is focused on the teacher delivering the subject knowledge, while the students listen and passively absorb subject information. Although similar to instructivist methodology, didactic methods are characteristic of low levels of student-teacher interaction while information transmission is focused on the teacher. Thus, while teachers actively transmit knowledge, the student's role is passive (i.e. listen and absorb) and teacher-student interaction is low.

Figure 2 illustrates the point at which knowledge is constructed – a central distinction between these methods of teaching. During student-centred activities, the student creates knowledge. During teacher-centred activities (e.g. instructivist-based teaching) knowledge is negotiated during student-teacher interaction. However, when didactic methods of teaching are employed, knowledge is created by the teacher and transmitted to the student. Because the methods of delivery between instructivist and didactic methods share similar characteristics, it

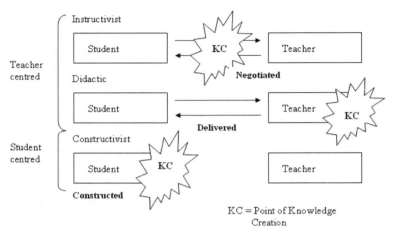

Figure 2 The point of knowledge creation

is probable that many educational researchers misinterpret traditional methods of instruction as instructivist-based methods when they are in fact didactic (lecture-style methods).

Marton and Booth (1997) have commented on the importance of interpersonal interaction between teachers and students. They argue that it requires a mutual awareness of the teaching-learning process and that the teachers need to 'mould experiences for their students with the aim of bringing about learning . . . the essential feature is that the teacher takes the part of the learner . . . the teacher focuses on the learner's experience of the object of learning' (p. 179).

Summary of main points

- The methods of teaching and the ways in which students perceive them affect the approach students take when studying.
- Biggs (1989) distinguishes between three separate 'conceptions of teaching': quantitative, institutional and qualitative.
- Those who take a quantitative view of teaching feel that teaching is the transmission of knowledge from the teacher to the student.

- Those who take an institutional view of teaching feel that teaching is the proficient orchestration of teaching skills.
- Those who take a qualitative view of teaching feel that teaching is the facilitation of learning.
- Constructivist-based and problem-based strategies are student-centred and focus on students as agents in the construction of their own knowledge rather than as active receptors of information in the classroom.
- The view that knowledge is not directly transmitted from the teacher to the student, but is actively built by the learner, underlies the basic premise of constructivist theories.
- A surface approach is characterized by unreflective rote memorization which students use when they need to simply reproduce information for an examination while a deep approach is characteristic of students who seek meaning and understanding by attempting to apply and compare ideas.
- What differentiates student-centred, instructivist and didactic methods of teaching is the point at which knowledge is created.

3 Learning in the FE classroom

The value of an education . . . is not the learning of many facts but the training of the mind to think something that cannot be learned from textbooks.

Albert Einstein

Conceptions of learning

Biggs (1989) distinguishes between three separate conceptions of learning: quantitative, institutional and qualitative. Students and teachers who have a quantitative view of learning feel that learning is a matter of 'how much' is learned. The curriculum is a seen as a collection of essential facts and skills to be taught, assimilated and tested. This attitude is evident in the philosophy underlying our current education system that is burdened by a stringent standardized testing regime and masses of examination board specifications. Students and teachers who take a quantitative view feel the purpose of assessment is to ensure coverage of the course content and feel that the purpose of learning is to absorb large amounts of information and facts.

Those who take an institutional view of learning feel that it should be validated by an educational establishment. Schools and colleges are the guardians of knowledge, while teachers are charged with teaching students that knowledge according to agreed procedures (e.g. examination boards and local education authority). The school or college has the authority to certify that students successfully completing courses have attained the requisite knowledge to be granted a qualification. This is another very predominant view of education amongst teachers and students in the FE sector. Students feel that their purpose for learning and studying is to obtain a qualification. This is not surprising, considering society's strong emphasis on attaining relevant qualifications. However, if students feel that the sole purpose of going to college is to obtain a qualification, what impact does this have on the perceptions of learning and teaching and the perceived value of education in this country?

Finally, those who take a qualitative view of learning feel that learning is a way of interpreting the world. Knowledge is constructed by learners, based on prior knowledge, which forms a framework through which they interpret and experience the world. Teachers who take a qualitative approach to learning will teach in ways that encourage problem–solving and critical thinking (Entwistle 1994).

Students' approaches to learning and studying

Students' and teachers' views of learning do have a great impact on the education system and the teaching and learning that occurs in the classroom. While there are many definitions of learning and studying, a predominant view of learning regards it as a cognitive process of acquiring new concepts, skills or knowledge or a process that brings about a change in behaviour as a result of experience. The concepts of learning and studying are often used interchangeably; this book, however, looks at studying as one method of learning. In the 1970s Marton and his colleagues in Gothenburg (Marton and Booth 1997; Marton, Hounsell and Entwistle 1997) used naturalistic experiments to identify qualitative differences in the ways in which students went about the task of reading an academic article (Marton and Säljö 1976, 1997).

Marton and Säljö's original work on approaches to studying (1976) explored students' approaches to learning a particular task. Students were given a subject text to read and were told that they would subsequently be asked questions on that text. The first group adopted an approach where they tried to understand the whole picture and tried to comprehend and understand the text whereas the second group tried to remember facts and focused on what they thought they would be asked later on a test. The central distinction that developed was a difference between 'deep' and 'surface' approaches to studying. The approach depended on the students' intentions and motives and on their perceptions of the task demands. The decision to seek meaning (deep) or to reproduce the information provided (surface) was seen as a consequence of how students had interpreted the task, the learning context and how they viewed the subject content.

What this means is that how students study for a subject is largely influenced by the method of teaching they experience, their views of learning (i.e. quantitative or qualitative) and the type of task (e.g. multiple choice test, short answer test or essay question) they are presented with. This research began to explain why students will rote memorize definitions and subject knowledge and facts when studying for a short answer test and why they will engage deeper with the information when they are studying for a final exam that is in an essay format. Since this pioneering work (Marton and Säljö 1976), the research on students' approaches to studying has explored the relationship between the teaching–learning environment (broadly defined to include teaching, assessment, learning materials, etc.) and student learning outcomes. I have found similar relationships between these internal and external factors to exist in further education (Weyers 2005).

'Deep', 'surface' and 'strategic' approaches to studying

The categories of deep and surface approaches to studying (Marton and Säljö 1976, 1997) were further elaborated with an approach to studying described as 'strategic' (Entwistle and Ramsden 1983) or 'achieving' (Biggs 1987). These approaches describe the different ways in which students approach their academic work and explain how different teaching and assessment methods affect those approaches. However, although students may take a 'deep' or 'surface' approach to their learning, these classifications are not personal attributes or learning styles and a student may use both approaches at different times depending on the learning environment.

'Deep' and 'surface' approaches to study have been identified in a number of studies (Biggs 1989; Entwistle and Ramsden

1983; Entwistle, McCune and Hounsell 2002). Students adopt an approach to studying that is affected by the learning environment (teaching methods, school expectations); their personal attributes (e.g. conceptions of learning) and the learning outcomes (e.g. obtaining a qualification, remembering or understanding subject information) they wish to achieve. While a surface approach is characterized by unreflective rote memorization with the purpose of reproducing information (e.g. on a standardized test), a deep approach is characterized by seeking meaning and understanding by applying and comparing ideas (e.g. transferring knowledge and skills to another context or situation). Surface approaches to studying employ reproductive strategies (e.g. rote memorization) to memorize information, with limited attention paid to the integration of newly acquired knowledge. A student using a surface approach to studying, which is considered unreflective and passive, concentrates on memorizing the material with limited attention paid to understanding the information (Marton and Säljö 1976, 1997; Thomas and Bain 1984).

There is a third approach to learning and studying known as the 'achieving' or 'strategic' approach, which can be described as a very well-organized form of a 'surface' approach to studying in which the motivation to learn is 'achieve something' (e.g. good grades to get into university). In this situation, learning can be seen as a game and achieving a good grade is the equivalent to winning (Atherton 2005b). This approach is very common in further education and describes an approach most FE teachers will recognize from their experiences in the classroom. It is not surprising, either, that our students take a strategic approach to their learning because their progression to higher education and future career opportunities is largely dependent on their ability to do well in college.

However, the research has shown that deep approaches produce optimal learning outcomes, while surface approaches are seen to be inadequate. Deep approaches to studying produce high-level learning outcomes and give students the ability to demonstrate their understanding of material (Whelan 1988; Balla *et al.* 1990; Trigwell and Sleet 1990); develop their conceptions of material (Van Rossum and Schenk 1984; Prosser and Millar 1989); and achieve higher grades (Entwistle and Ramsden 1983; Ramsden et al. 1986; Eley 1992; Drew and Watkins 1998).

While surface approaches involve the routine use of rote memorization and deep approaches are characteristic of making connections with previous knowledge and carrying out logical reasoning (Entwistle and Smith 2002), research with Chinese learners has shown that the link between memorization and the surface approach appears to be an oversimplification (Kember 1996; Watkins and Biggs 1996). Where memorization involves meaningful learning, it has been described as 'deep memorizing' (Tang 1991) or 'memorizing with understanding', an approach also displayed by British students (Meyer 2000). The main element of a surface approach is not rote memorization but the routine and unreflective use of information, which stems from the intention to simply reproduce the material presented by the teacher (Entwistle and Smith 2002).

Recent research has begun to make it clear that a student's approach to studying and their perceptions of the teaching they experience are two of the most direct influences on the quality of the learning they achieve (Prosser and Trigwell 1999). Further, student's prior educational experiences are reflected in their conceptions of learning (Säljö 1979; Marton and Säljö 1997) and also in their reasons for studying and their learning orientations (Beaty et al. 1997). This suggests that the educational experiences that students have in secondary school will be a strong influence on the way that they view learning (i.e. quantitative or qualitative) and the way that they approach their studying. Therefore, students enter FE with strongly entrenched study habits and opinions about the nature of learning.

Vermunt (1998) found that students bring to any course 'baggage' that takes the form of previous education, knowledge and understanding and this baggage influences how they make sense of the subject matter and how they study. Further, in my previous study (Weyers 2005) I found that students enter further education with firmly established study habits from secondary school which may be inappropriate for post-compulsory education. In addition, students will attempt to interpret the learning situation in terms of their previous experience in which teachers in secondary school may, or may not, have provided extremely structured guidance on what work to do, what information to learn and to what depth. When they enter FE, they assume that teachers will still provide their education packaged for them on a platter. When they do not, it causes students a great deal of anxiety.

The research on teaching and learning suggests that deep approaches to studying are related to what students perceive as 'good teaching', while a heavy workload is linked to a surface approach. This means that when our students are feeling the demands of coursework compounded with the stress of examinations, they tend to take a surface approach (i.e. rote memorization strategies) to studying. Furthermore, the research suggests that some assessment methods, such as multiple-choice questions and short answer tests, tend to induce surface approaches to studying (Scouller 1998), while more open forms of assessment (essay-type and authentic problems) encourage deep approaches to studying. This is worrying, considering the prevalence of short answer examinations in further education.

Some researchers suggest that it is a student's perception of the teaching and assessment procedures, rather than the methods themselves, that affect student study strategies most directly (Ramsden 1997; Entwistle 1998a, b). Therefore, even though as teachers we may design learning tasks and in-class assessments to encourage a deep approach to learning and studying, it is our student's perception of the task, rather than the task itself, that will encourage or discourage students to take a deep approach.

Lizzio et al. (2002) argue that the perception of having a heavy workload (the amount of coursework and assignments students are expected to complete) influences students to adopt a surface or reproducing approach to study. When Fransson (1977) set out experimentally to induce different approaches to studying by varying the context, he found that students who reported anxiety were more likely to adopt a surface approach, while those who saw the subject context as interesting adopted a deep approach to reading. What is troubling for us is that many of our students leave studying until examination time and the majority of our students feel a great stress during this period.

It is not surprising then that many of our students take a surface approach to their studying to deal with the pressure of succeeding.

During my previous study (Weyers 2005), I found that students find it difficult to manage the increased workload demands and the amount of independent learning they are expected to engage in when they enter non-compulsory FE. Working within the constraints of a standardized curriculum and examination board specifications with internal and external pressure to cover large syllabuses, it is not surprising that teachers feel the pressure to adapt their teaching to ensure that their students succeed. In these situations, we often revert to a transmission model of teaching to ensure that we have covered all the required information despite the fact that we know there are more effective, enriching and innovative ways to teach.

Critical thinking in the FE classroom

Critical thinking is the process students use to reflect on and judge the assumptions underlying their own and others' ideas and actions. It is a complex activity and while it is possible to teach critical thinking as a repertoire of separate skills, these skills are best developed in relation to a domain of knowledge (e.g. biology, physics) (Carr 1990). Thus, it is crucial that we create a learning environment that encourages students to use these skills.

Bloom *et al.* (1956) proposed that knowing is composed of six successive levels: knowledge, comprehension, application, analysis, synthesis and evaluation. He designed *The Taxonomy of the Cognitive Domain* which outlined six hierarchical levels of educational outcomes. Krathwol and Anderson's (2000) revision of Bloom's *Taxonomy of Educational Objectives* can be used as a tool to help formulate learning outcomes. The taxonomy identifies six levels of thinking (and associated cognitive processes) that students will engage in when asked to do particular activities in the classroom (learning tasks, assignments, queries from the teacher). Table 1 outlines a revision of Bloom's taxonomy of educational objectives. This taxonomy can be used as a guide for creating effective questions during class discussions

Table 1 A taxonomy of learning for teaching: A revision of Bloom's taxonomy of educational objectives

Aims	Outcomes
Remember	Recognize, recall, identify, retrieve, name
Understand	Interpret, paraphrase, translate, represent, clarify Exemplify, instantiate, illustrate Classify, categorize, subsume Summarize, abstract, generalize Infer, extrapolate, interpolate, predict, conclude Compare, contrast, match, map Explain, construct models
Apply	Execute, carry out Implement, use
Analyse	Differentiate, discriminate, select, distinguish, focus Organize, outline, structure, integrate, find coherence, parse Attribute, deconstruct
Evaluate	Check, test, detect, monitor, co-ordinate Critique, judge
Create	Generate, hypothesize Plan, design Produce, construct

(Taken from Wilkinson *et al.* (n.d.) 'Aims and learning outcomes' which was adapted from Krathwol and Anderson (2000) *A Taxonomy of Learning for Teaching: A Revision of Bloom's Taxonomy of Educational Objectives.*)

that encourage higher-level learning outcomes (e.g. analysis, evaluation) and can also be used for creating assessment questions to test higher-level learning (e.g. by asking students to 'hypothesize' or 'construct').

Implications for the classroom

Critical to our understanding of student learning is our acceptance that students do not have a fixed approach to learning but rather that they adopt a particular approach in

Table 2 Definitions, characteristics and suggestions for practice

Definitions

Deep approach	Examining new facts and ideas critically, tying them into existing cognitive structures and making numerous links between ideas.
Surface approach	Accepting new facts and ideas uncritically and attempting to store them as isolated, unconnected items.

Characteristics of approach are:

Deep	• looking for meaning • focusing on the central argument or *concepts* needed to solve a problem • interacting actively • distinguishing between argument and evidence • making connections between different modules • relating new and previous knowledge • linking course content to real life
Surface	• relying on rote learning • focusing on outwards signs and the *formulae* needed to solve a problem • receiving information passively • failing to distinguish principles from examples • treating parts of modules and programmes as separate • not recognising new material as building on previous work • seeing course content simply as material to be learnt for the exam.

Characteristics of student
Students will take a deep/surface approach if they:

Deep	• have an intrinsic curiosity in the subject • are determined to do well and mentally engage when doing their work • have the appropriate background knowledge for a sound foundation • through good time management have time to pursue their interests • have a positive experience of education leading to confidence in their ability to understand and succeed.

Table 2 *continued*

Surface	• are studying for a qualification when they are not interested in the subject • are not focusing on their academic life and emphasizing other interests (e.g. social, sport) • lack the background knowledge necessary to understand material • do not have enough time/too heavy a workload • have a cynical view of education and believe that factual recall is what is required • have high anxiety.

Encouraged by teachers
An approach can be encouraged by teachers if they:

Deep	• show personal interest in the subject • bring out the structure of the subject • concentrate on and ensure plenty of time for key concepts • confront students' misconceptions and engage students in active learning • use assessments that require thought, and require ideas to be used together • relate new material to what students already know and understand • allow students to make mistakes without penalty, and reward effort • are consistent and fair in assessing the intended learning outcomes, and by doing so establish trust
Surface	• convey disinterest or even a negative attitude to the material • present the material so that it can be perceived as a series of unrelated facts and ideas • allow students to be passive • assess for independent facts (short answer questions) • rush to cover too much material • emphasize coverage at the expense of depth • create undue anxiety or low expectations of success by discouraging statements or excessive workload • have a short assessment cycle.

(Taken from the Engineering Subject Centre of the HEA; www.engsc.ac.uk/er/theory/learning.asp.)

response to their experience in the classroom. Table 2, adapted for the FE context (taken from the Engineering Subject Centre of the Higher Education Academy (HEA)), outlines the characteristics of these approaches and provides some suggestions for teachers based on the work of Biggs (1999) and Ramsden (1992). For example, clearly stated academic aims, opportunities to exercise some choice and well-aligned assessment strategies that help students to build confidence can be found among the factors identified as encouraging a deep approach. Similarly, over-assessment through repeated testing will encourage a surface approach while fewer assessments and assessments that require students to engage with problems will encourage them to use and apply their learning and facilitate a deep approach.

Students need to remember the basic facts and subject information before they can begin to understand more complex subject matter within a domain of knowledge. While this does not suggest that competence in a domain occurs in a simple linear fashion, it does suggest that engaging with the information and applying it will undoubtedly lead to a deeper understanding of the subject. If students attempt to apply complex principles without a good solid grasp of the basic fundamental principles from which they are built, they will only end up frustrated and begin to rote-memorize complex subject matter that they cannot understand (Engineering Subject Centre–HEA 2005).

Suggestions teachers can make to students to improve their learning

The ways students reflect on and monitor their own learning influences their beliefs about teaching and learning. The following are some suggestions teachers can make to their students to improve their learning (based on McCune 2003, p. 3)

Students should try to:

- make an effort to understand ideas themselves
- make links between the subject topics
- relate what is learned to the wider world

- look for the patterns and underlying principles of what they are learning
- check the evidence and relate it to conclusions that are drawn
- examine the logic of the arguments made critically
- become actively interested in the course content.

Students should try not to:

- only cope minimally with course requirements
- treat the subject as a mass of unrelated bits of knowledge
- memorize subject information without attempting to understand it
- accept subject information and ideas without questioning them.

Many students in FE have been coached by their teachers to pass examinations largely by completing past examination papers. They are told what types of questions to expect and how to answer those questions. They have been trained to be surface learners because memorizing subject information is all that is required to pass the examination. The experience of students and teachers alike is that these methods work and it is not surprising that they continue to use such strategies.

Summary of main points

- Deep approaches to learning and studying are related to what students perceive as good teaching.
- A heavy workload is linked to a surface approach.

As teachers we should:

- teach in a way that encourages students to adopt a deep approach
- show personal interest in the subject
- bring out the structure of the subject
- concentrate on and ensure plenty of time for key concepts
- confront students' misconceptions and engage students in active learning

- use assessments that require thought, and require ideas to be used together
- relate new material to what students already know and understand
- allow students to make mistakes without penalty, and reward effort
- be consistent and fair in assessing the intended learning outcomes, and by doing so establish trust.

4 Curriculum design for deep learning

I never teach my pupils; I only attempt to provide the conditions in which they can learn.

Albert Einstein

This chapter will cover some of the central principles teachers should take into consideration when designing the curriculum and will describe some techniques that are important if you are trying to design an effective learning environment that maximizes student engagement and focuses on understanding rather than simple rote learning. There are three central considerations that FE teachers need to incorporate into their classrooms:

1. *Mapping students' initial knowledge to target knowledge* – You need to provide opportunities for students to see the link between what they already know and what they are learning.

2. *Integrating and making links across the curriculum* – The subject specification outlines modular topics; however, you need to provide students with the opportunity to see clearly the links that exist between these various subject topics.

3. *Linking course modules and creating a holistic understanding of the course* – The course should be designed in a way that allows students to see the links between the separate course modules/units. Most academic and vocational courses are split into separate modules for assessment purposes. However, students need to see that these are not separate chunks of information but are interrelated topics that share multiple connections. Often teaching an FE course in a non-modular format can reduce this problem; however, when it comes to final examinations,

students will need to understand what topics they will be tested on in each module examination.

'Personal understanding' versus 'target understanding'

Smith (1998) used Scottish Higher Biology (age 17+) to describe the process that an examination board goes through when designing examination documents by illustrating the ways in which an official syllabus is designed and communicated to teachers. He describes target understanding as a selection of topics and ideas from a universe of knowledge that exists within each subject area. He goes on to explain that when the syllabus is constructed, topics need to be described and learning specifications set that outline the required level of understanding students should be expected to reach. He points out that these targets are constructed by board experts based on their conceptualizations of the subject and written into formalized statements following consultations and comments from schools (i.e. examination board subject specifications).

Smith draws a distinction between 'target understanding' and 'personal understanding'. He argues that 'target understanding' reflects the targets set by the teacher derived from the formal requirements of the curriculum, whereas 'personal understanding' reflects the students' conception of the topic, which is filtered through the teaching methods and the student's prior education and personal experience. Smith explains that the target understanding experienced by students is also filtered through the teacher's understanding of the subject and communicated by the teacher through comments and explanations while in the classroom. Smith argues that this distillation process inevitably leaves student's personal understanding of the target knowledge 'hazy' and inhibits their ability to achieve the level of understanding expected by the examination board. Further, elaborating on Smith's idea, while the prescriptive nature of these specifications was intended to guide the design of subject examinations, it is probable that teachers adjust their teaching to the syllabus specifications and align their teaching to the methods of assessment and level of understanding that is typically expected in examinations (e.g. low-level learning outcomes such as 'describe the . . .' or 'list the five . . .').

However, teachers can enhance the quality of their teaching and the subsequent learning that takes place in the FE classroom by employing alternative teaching strategies that produce deeper levels of student engagement. Teachers need to be aware of the unconscious messages that they may impart in the classroom. For example, by setting learning tasks in the classroom that only ask students to describe or list subject information, they are unintentionally telling the student that they only need to engage with the course on a descriptive level to pass the examination. As Biggs (1989) points out, often assessment practices are interpreted by students in ways that may be unexpected by teachers; teachers need to be aware of these subtleties that influence a student's choice of study strategies.

Thus, while 'target understanding' is derived from the formal requirements of the syllabus interpreted through the teacher, 'personal understanding' reflects a student's conception of the topic that has been formed through the delivery of the topic by the teacher. As FE teachers we need to understand the prescriptive nature of examination board specifications and attempt to 'go beyond the words' of the syllabus to encourage higher-level learning outcomes (e.g. problem-solving, critical thinking).

What is constructive alignment?

Difficulties can also occur when tasks set by teachers are misunderstood by students (Entwistle and Smith 2002). Constructive alignment challenges teachers to think critically about the alignment in their classes between course aims, teaching, learning tasks and assessment. The term 'constructive' implies a constructivist approach that suggests course aims should focus on a 'deep' level of understanding and high-quality learning. Constructive alignment is the combination of constructivist theory and aligned instruction (Biggs 2003).

Course aims are outlined clearly in examination board specifications for all courses in the FE sector. All FE teachers are well aware of the specifications that cover their courses. What is not widely recognized in FE course design is the fact that the teaching and assessment procedures may still create a mismatch that is not recognized by teachers or students. For example, examination specifications that state students should attain a high-level learning outcome such as 'understanding' cannot use didactic lecture-style teaching to teach students to 'understand' subject information and proceed to test for this learning outcome by a short answer test. However, the predominant method of teaching is still the information transmission model and short answer tests still dominate many subject examinations in the FE sector.

This would suggest that much of the curriculum in many FE subjects is not constructively aligned. Most examination specifications outline the topics teachers should 'cover' and curriculum textbooks outline clearly to the teacher what students need to know about the topic. Rote-memorizing subject information to regurgitate during an exam does not require students to demonstrate their understanding. However, what would you think of a medical school that only lectured on surgical medicine and assessed their doctor's competence based on an essay? Some may argue that coursework modules exist for students to demonstrate their application of subject knowledge. However, teachers who have taught these modules are well aware of the prescriptive nature of the way that coursework has been traditionally taught in FE. Often, teachers teaching coursework modules feel the pressure to guide their students to complete the work correctly because they feel their student's failure is a reflection on their teaching.

Further, the modular approach of many academic and vocational courses tends to be perceived by students as segmented and unrelated units of information rather than as a coherent whole. If we want our students to demonstrate their understanding at the appropriate level, teaching modules need to be properly aligned with coursework modules and the teaching and assessment need to reflect high-level learning outcomes. Short of calling for a restructuring of academic and vocational courses in FE and the revision of the examination specifications and testing procedures, teachers can begin to constructively align the courses they teach using the SOLO Taxonomy (Biggs 2003).

The SOLO taxonomy

SOLO stands for the Structure of the Observed Learning Outcome and is a means of classifying learning outcomes in terms of their complexity. It was first developed by Biggs and Collis (1982) and is well described in Biggs (2003). It is largely applicable to any subject area and is a useful tool for implementing constructive alignment. It describes, through five stages, the level of increasing complexity in a student's understanding of a subject (Atherton 2005c). Of course, not all students get through all five stages and this can be partly because of the teaching, method of assessment or both.

At first, when learners only pick up a few aspects of the course content, they have a 'unistructural' understanding of the subject. As they progress through the course, they begin to recall more information and facts, but the information and facts are unrelated ('multistructural' understanding). When students learn how to integrate subject information into a coherent whole and see the relationship between the different topics and subtopics, they begin to have a 'relational' understanding of the subject or course. Finally, if they start to generalize that conceptual understanding to other knowledge domains or show untaught applications of the information, they have an 'extended abstract' understanding. Unfortunately, the majority of students in FE will not attain this level of understanding and most will not even attain a relational understanding of the subject we are teaching them. However, this is not to say that they cannot.

The emphasis within this framework of making connections and contextualizing information links well with Marton and Säljö's (1976) approaches to studying (deep and surface), and Biggs' (1989) conceptions of learning and constructivist theories of learning and teaching. Further, similar to Bloom's taxonomy (Bloom 1956) the model assumes that each level builds in complexity from the previous level. Table 3 outlines the SOLO levels and the description of the task that teachers can use to encourage students to reach a particular level of understanding (Biggs 2003).

Constructive alignment (Biggs 2003) is the process of taking a strategic and integrated approach to curriculum design by

Table 3 SOLO levels and descriptions

SOLO level	Task description
Prestructural	Student misses the point
Unistructural	Identify, do simple procedure
Multistructural	Enumerate, describe, list, combine, do algorithms
Relational	Compare/contrast, explain causes, analyse, relate, apply
Extended abstract	Theorize, generalize, hypothesize, reflect

(Adapted from Biggs (2003) p. 48).

strategically aligning curriculum objectives, teaching methods and assessment methods to meet the same high-level learning outcomes. Effective teaching within this framework requires that high-level learning outcomes (e.g. problem solving, critical thinking) are addressed both by the teaching methods and by the assessment tasks (Biggs 1996). While we cannot control the examination boards, as teachers we can control what learning tasks, teaching methods and formative assessment (e.g. homework assignments) we use to encourage high-level learning outcomes.

Implications for the classroom

Three fundamental tenets underlie this strategy:

1. The overall process of learning is built on a framework of curriculum design in which the intended learning outcomes, teaching methods and assessment are inter-dependent and only by integrating these elements of the curriculum can you achieve optimum learning outcomes.
2. Teachers need to reflect critically on their curricular design and be prepared to change and adapt to meet the changing needs of the learners.
3. Understanding cannot be transmitted from the teacher to the student but must be actively constructed by the student.

Smith (1998) explains that the target understanding experienced by students is filtered further through the teacher's understanding of the subject and communicated through comments and explanations made by the teacher over many occasions in the classroom. Smith explains that this process inevitably leaves the student's understanding of the target knowledge 'hazy' and inhibits their ability to achieve the understanding expected by the teacher or examiner. My research (Weyers 2005) found that advanced subsidiary (AS) students studying at a sixth-form college felt they needed to learn the information twice: once to be competent to write the examination and a second time to understand the topic and its application to the real world.

This suggests that there needs to be a degree of constructive alignment between assessment methods and the expected learning outcomes in lessons. Thus, the method of assessment should reflect the intended level and form of understanding that students are expected to achieve. If we are asking students to 'understand' the subject information, assessing that understanding using a short-answer or multiple-choice test is not adequate. Unfortunately, a large portion of the examinations in FE courses are still in this format.

As teachers, we need to have a clear idea of what we want our students to achieve and the level which we want them to reach. By clearly communicating these expectations to students, we allow them to take ownership for their own learning and share in the responsibility of achieving these goals. FE students have played the assessment game throughout their many years of formal schooling and they adapt their study strategies to mirror the type of assessment. Unfortunately, in FE we have no control over the type of assessment used for examinations. What we do have control over is the way that assessment is perceived by the students. Therefore, links need to be made between examination modules and coursework modules. This allows students to see a coherence and continuity between the modules rather than seeing modules as separate disparate bodies of knowledge that have no connection to each other.

The examination specifications are the learning outcomes for FE courses. Students need to see the links between the specifications and how they are interrelated. Further, formative (ongoing) assessment needs to encourage higher-level learning outcomes. This is the difficulty for constructively aligning courses in FE. Often the specifications use low-level learning outcomes (e.g. describe, state, list) which only encourage students to work at lower levels of competence.

However, to assist your students to achieve higher-level learning outcomes in your class, you will want to mix the levels of learning expected from your students and have some lower-level outcomes that deal with the basic facts and higher-level outcomes that require students to apply the information and knowledge. For example, for an A level physics course, you will expect students to state a fundamental physical law (low-level outcome); however, you may also want your students to understand how to apply the law (high-level outcome). Formative (ongoing) assessment can be used to assess these higher-level learning outcomes. For example, group work in class that encourages collaboration; class presentations that encourage students to demonstrate and explain a principle or concept to the rest of the class; or homework assignments that ask students to problem-solve, demonstrate and extrapolate using the core facts/knowledge of the subject.

Classroom activities/assessments need to encourage students to engage with the information and take an active role in their learning. If we want students to synthesize concepts and link them together, then we should consider assessment activities which encourage that behaviour. While coursework modules do attempt to do this, we need to link these modules more closely to the traditional examination modules. Teachers need to be confident enough to let students make mistakes and learn from them. Within these modules the 'learning process' needs to take precedence rather than the 'end product' that is produced. It is the process that allows students to develop their problem-solving and critical-thinking skills.

Finally, assessment comes in many forms (peer assessment, teacher assessment or individual/personal assessment) and is not always in the form of an examination solely used for grading purposes (although after teaching a few years in the FE sector it is difficult to believe otherwise). What is of paramount importance is that the assessment method (e.g. problem-based learning (PBL) case study) actually assesses the intended learning outcome (e.g. problem–solving, critical thinking). By focusing on higher-level learning outcomes and including these assessment methods into your classroom in a pedagogically sound manner, you have constructively aligned your course.

Summary of main points

- Teachers need to provide opportunities for students to see the link between what they already know and what they are learning.
- The subject specification outlines modular topics; however, you need to provide students with the opportunity to see clearly the links that exist between these various subject topics.
- A course should be designed in a way that allows students to see the links between the separate course modules/units.
- Teachers need to be aware of the unconscious messages that they may impart in the classroom.
- 'Target understanding' is derived from the formal requirements of the syllabus interpreted through the teacher; 'personal understanding' reflects a student's conception of the topic that has been formed through the delivery of the topic by the teacher.
- What is not widely recognized in FE course design is the fact that the teaching and assessment procedures may still create a mismatch that is not recognized by teachers or students.
- Constructive alignment (Biggs 2003) is the process of taking a strategic and integrated approach to curriculum design by strategically aligning curriculum objectives, teaching methods and assessment methods to meet the same high-level learning outcomes.
- Constructive alignment is a combination of constructivist theory and aligned instruction.
- What is of paramount importance is that the assessment method (e.g. PBL case study) actually assesses the intended learning outcomes (e.g. problem–solving, critical thinking).

5 Engaging students in the classroom

Most teachers waste their time by asking questions which are intended to discover what a pupil does not know whereas the true art of questioning has for its purpose to discover what the pupil knows or is capable of knowing.

Albert Einstein

Conversational approach to teaching

Socrates liked to work with students. His approach essentially consisted of leading them through a series of questions in order to promote critical thinking. On one occasion, the philosopher purportedly led a group of students to a difficult conclusion through his Socratic method. Socrates then pointed out that, since he had reported no facts, the students must have known the conclusion all along.
(Taken from Murphy (1997) *Constructivism: From Philosophy to Practice*; www.cdli.ca/~elmurphy/emurphy/cle.html.)

The conversational approach is a model of learning and teaching based on the processes that underpin learner–teacher interaction. While some models are student-centred and focus on learning as an experience that changes the learner and others are teacher-centred and focus on the teacher and the method of instruction, Laurillard's (1993) conversational model looks at the process of interaction between the teacher and the student. Laurillard argues that it is the process of negotiation between the teacher and the student which transforms the learners' understanding of a topic (Atherton 2005a).

To some extent, conversational theories of learning take a cognitive constructivist perspective because of the emphasis on the learner as an active participant in the construction of knowledge. The teacher's role in this learning process is to maintain a dialogue with the learner to assist him/her in refining their understanding until it is more closely aligned with that of the teacher (ibid.). This process attempts to align a student's personal understanding with a teacher's target understanding (Smith 1998) and resembles a form of active scaffolding whereby the teacher interacts with the student to encourage them to think and develop their conceptions of a topic or subject.

The process of the learning conversation

Atherton (2005a) outlines Laurillard's (1993) pattern of conversation:

---

1. The teacher sets the task/goal.
2. The teacher describes his/her conception of the subject.
3. The learner then replies by describing his/her conception of the topic.
4. The teacher can re-describe in the light of the learner's conception.
5. The learner can re-describe in the light of the teacher's re-description.
6. The teacher can adapt the task goal in the light of the learner's description or action.
7. And so on...

(Based on Laurillard (1993).)

Laurillard states that for this model to work the following features need to be present (as stated in Atherton 2005a):

1. The teacher sets the task.
2. The learner can act to achieve the task goal.
3. The teacher can 'set up the world' (i.e. control the learning environment) to give intrinsic feedback on actions.
4. The learner can modify his/her action in the light of feedback.
5. The learner can modify his/her action in the light of the teacher's description or his/her (the learner's) re-description.
6. The learner can reflect on interaction to modify re-description.
7. The teacher can reflect on the learner's action to modify re-description

(Based on Laurillard (1993, p. 119). Note that this has been slightly modified in the 2nd edn.)

Techniques for starting a discussion

The questions that you ask to initiate discussions in the classroom are key to successfully engaging students in critical thinking that can deepen their engagement with the information and motivate them to develop their own views and opinions. Experienced teachers prepare a mix of questions ranging from easily answered to highly complex. To engage students in higher-order thinking you need to ask questions that require students to explain relationships among the units of information and to form general concepts. Alternatively, ask questions that require students to apply the concepts they have learnt to new situations.

The following are strategies used for starting a discussion (adapted from Frederick (1981) for the FE classroom):

1. *Concept mapping* – Ask each student in the class to state a key point they picked up from the teaching sessions or their course readings. Make a list and ask students to identify the connections that emerge between the different themes. Show the connections between the themes by drawing lines between the information/ concepts and the missing elements. A mind map of concepts/topics can be developed on the front board and discussed with the class. At the end of the academic year, give copies of the examination subject specifications to students to assist them with making connections between the important topics/elements of the course. This will allow students to see how the various topics that have been covered throughout the year fit together.

2. *Generating questions* – Ask students to generate questions based on their course readings or the lesson you have just finished. Use different methods to brainstorm questions and incorporate them into a class discussion. After getting students to generate answers for some lower-level question (e.g. describe, list), reword some of the questions to encourage more complex thinking (e.g. reflect on . . ., compare and contrast . . .). Allow students to form groups and ask each other questions.

3. *Illustrative quotations* – Ask each student to find one or two quotations from the course readings that he/she found best illustrated the major concepts discussed in the teaching session or the readings. Discuss these quotes in small groups or as a class and show how they relate to other concepts and topics discussed in previous weeks of the course. Students can create mind maps using their quotations as starting points and extrapolate new quotations that represent connecting concepts.

4. *Breakout groups* – To discuss various issues or course concepts, have students form small groups at the start or end of the lesson. Keep instructions clear and simple and ensure discussions focus specifically on the

subject's examination subject specifications. You can vary the way that groups are formed and the ways that groups report back and summarize what they have discussed. It is useful to pick a different topic each week and list the examination specifications on the front board. Different groups can then discuss different specifications and report to the class a summary of their discussion.

5. *Truth statements* – Have students decide upon two or three statements that they know to be true about a particular subject topic or concept. Allow them to use their textbook or course notes. Use this as a starting point to initiate a critical discussion around the topic. Use the truth statements as starting points to emphasize that there are always exceptions, things are not always black and white, and that truth is often subjective.

6. *Debate* – Present students with an argument that has two sides. In groups, the students use the subject information (textbooks, course notes, the Internet) to gain evidence to support their position. Students take part in a debate and are each given two minutes to present their points. The teacher acts as a group moderator to ensure only one student talks at a time and the discussion keeps flowing. Alternatively, ask students to select one or the other of two opposite sides and defend their choice. Ask them to sit on one side of a table or room to represent their decision. Ask why they have chosen to sit where they are. Invite students to feel free to change their place during a debate.

7. *Non-structured scene-setting* – Stay out of the discussion, provide a prompt (slide, quote, audio recording) and allow students to discuss a course topic.

(Adapted from Frederick (1981))

Ways to discourage student participation in discussions

Sometimes when teaching you find yourself standing at the front of a class doing most of the talking and answering your own questions. It is during these monologues that students often disengage and the teacher realizes the majority of their students are silent and motionless. Further, when students do talk, they invariably address their remarks to the teacher rather than to each other, and there is no genuine dialogue between students in the class. Try to avoid situations where one student dominates the discussion. Although the active dialogue between yourself and the eager student may be beneficial to that student, the other students in the class will disengage and feel what is being discussed is of no concern to them. In such situations, it is often useful to direct the student's question to other students in the class. This subtle gesture implies to students that the focus of the classroom is not you (the teacher) and that questions raised are the responsibility of all in the classroom.

Another common problem that arises in FE classrooms is when students insist on being given the 'correct answers' without discussion, debate or explanation. Students often do not care about how to find the solution to a problem, rather, they want to know what the answer is so that they can memorize it in the event that a similar question arises in an examination. The problem with this scenario is two-fold. Students who take this approach often adopt rote-memorization strategies when studying rather than focusing on engaging at a deeper level with the information. They also neglect the process of learning and the transferable skills (e.g. problem-solving, critical thinking) that develop when answering subject-based questions. In these situations, it is difficult for novice teachers not to fall into the trap of simply providing the correct answers. However, if students are to develop independent thinking skills, the process of learning needs to be demonstrated in class, practised by students and modelled by you (the teacher).

Other potential pitfalls and ways to avoid them are as follows (Biggs 2003):

1. *Insufficient wait time* – When you answer questions too quickly, you do not allow students to sufficiently engage with the question and begin to construct their thoughts around an answer. Increasing the wait time from one second to three to five seconds has been shown to increase the length and number of appropriate responses received. The uncomfortable silence that may occur when lengthening the wait time may seem awkward but will quickly become a normal aspect of class discussions.

2. *The rapid reward* – A response such as '*Right . . . good*' to a student's comment and moving on to the next topic during a discussion gives the impression to students that further thinking should be terminated. This type of behaviour favours students that are fast thinkers and may actually be biased against students who think more deeply and have longer processing times.

3. *The programmed answer* – Questions such as 'Why doesn't . . .?' or 'It has . . . doesn't it?' are questions that answer themselves. When you answer your own questions, it gives the message to students that you have little interest in what they have to say. It also deprives students from constructing and expressing their thoughts on the matter.

4. *Non-specific feedback questions* – You will often hear teachers at the end of class ask, 'Does anyone have any questions?' what this question is actually asking students is if they understand everything that was covered in the lesson. For a student to raise their hand and ask a question is equivalent to admitting their ignorance. This final question is problematic however, because if you maintain a classroom in which students know and trust you they will feel safe to show their misunderstandings. Therefore, this rule does not always apply.

Questions that promote learning

In any subject area, the level of questioning influences the depth of thinking that occurs between the teacher and student. For example, if students are asked to simply state or describe a basic definition or fact within a domain of knowledge then the response will be simply recalled from memory. Thought-provoking questions require students to go beyond facts and use knowledge (critically analyse, reflect) to make judgements. A good question is one that challenges student understanding and requires analysis, synthesis, interpretation and critical thinking in order to answer it. Table 4 (adapted from Stanford University, Centre for Learning and Teaching 2004) outlines some types of questions that tend to facilitate thoughtful sustained discussions:

Table 4 Questions that promote high-level learning outcomes

Questions that promote learning high-level learning outcomes	
1. Analysis	Questions beginning with 'Why . . .?', 'How would you explain . . .?', 'What is the importance of . . .?', 'What is the meaning of. . .?'
2. Compare and contrast	'Compare . . .', 'Contrast . . .', 'What is the difference between . . .?', 'What is the similarity between . . .?'
3. Cause and effect	'What are the causes/results of . . .?', 'What connection is there between . . .'
4. Clarification	'What is meant by . . .?', 'Explain how . . .'
Questions that do not promote learning	
5. Simple Yes/No Produces little discussion and encourages guessing.	'Is the sky blue?'
6. Elliptical Too vague; it is not clear what is being asked.	'Well, what do you think about the characters' values and opinions?'
7. Leading Conveys the expected answer.	'Using that technique to calculate the solution is an effective technique, isn't it?'

(Taken from Stanford University, Centre for Teaching and Learning (2004) 'Designing effective discussion questions'.)

Socratic questioning to encourage high-level learning outcomes

A teacher's use of probing questions when facilitating inquiry and critical thinking is an essential component of learning in the classroom. Socratic questioning encourages reflection and critical, convergent and divergent thinking and promotes synthesis of information into discernible categories of 'fact' and 'opinion'. Paul (1993) argues that the strategic use of questioning is meant to help learners arrive at judgements that are based on their own reasoning and recognize assumptions, implications, concepts, consequences and alternative points of view which are all considered to be important elements of higher-order thinking.

Socratic questioning is not based on a set format or sequence of questioning but includes a taxonomy of questions that can be used when a teacher facilitates critical thinking. Stepien (1999b) points out six areas of Socratic questioning:

- probing assumptions;
- probing clarification;
- probing for reasons and evidence;
- revealing differing viewpoints and perspectives;
- probing implications and/or consequences;
- questions for responding to questions.

Paul outlines a taxonomy of Socratic questions that build upon each other but are not confined to a set pattern. One question's response will lead into another. The role of the teacher in a class discussion is to keep the inquiry focused but allow students to arrive at conclusions based on their own critical analysis and reasoning. Table 5 outlines some examples of Socratic questions that can be used in class discussions to facilitate high-level learning outcomes.

Table 5 Socratic questioning to facilitate high-level learning during class discussions

Questions of clarification

'Why do you say that?', 'How does this relate to our discussion?', 'What do you mean by ...?', 'Could you put that another way?', 'What do you think is the main issue in ...?', 'What do you take ... to mean by his/her remark?', 'Can you summarize in your own words what ... said?'

Questions that probe assumptions

'What could we assume instead about ...?', 'How can you verify or disprove that assumption?', 'What is ... assuming?', 'All of your reasoning depends on the idea that ... Why have you based your reasoning on ... instead of ...?', 'You seem to be assuming ... Is that always the case?'

Questions that probe reasons and evidence

'What would be an example?', 'What do you think causes ... to happen?', 'Why?', 'Why do you think that is true?', 'What are your reasons for saying that?', 'Is there a reason to doubt the evidence?', 'Can someone else provide evidence to support that view?', 'What reasoning brought you to that conclusion?'

Questions about viewpoints or perspectives

'What would be an alternative?', 'What is another way of looking at it?', 'Would you explain why it is necessary or beneficial, and who benefits?', 'Why is this best?', 'What are the strengths and weaknesses of ...?', 'How are ... and ... similar?', 'What is a counterargument for ...?'

'Questions that probe implications and consequences

'What generalizations can you make about that?', 'What are you implying when you say that?', 'How does ... affect ...?', 'How does ... tie in with what we learned ...?', 'Is this the same as. .?', 'Why is this issue important?', 'Is this the most important question, or are there underlying questions that are really the issue?'

(Adapted from Stepien (1999a) which was originally adapted from Paul (1993).)

Summary of main points

- Avoid giving a lecture and talking too much rather than conducting a dialogue.
- Do not allow a single student to dominate the discussion.
- Avoid simply giving students answers/solutions to class problems. Rather, have the class discuss possible solutions/ answers.
- Do not allow students to simply respond to you. Rather, create an atmosphere where students take part in discussions and respond to questions by directing their answers to the entire class.
- When leading a discussion prepare a mix of questions (easily answered, mildly challenging, highly complex).
- A teacher's use of probing questions when facilitating inquiry and critical thinking is an essential component of learning in the classroom.
- A good question is one that challenges student understanding and requires analysis, synthesis, interpretation and critical thinking in order to answer it.
- When leading a discussion, ask questions requiring students to explain relationships among the units of information and to form general concepts.
- Ask questions that require students to apply concepts they have developed to new data and different situations.
- The teacher's role in this learning process is to maintain a dialogue with the learner to assist him/her in refining their understanding until it is more closely aligned with that of the teacher.
- When you answer questions too quickly you do not allow students to sufficiently engage with the question.
- A rapid reward response to a student's answer favours students who are fast thinkers but may actually be biased against students who think more deeply and have longer processing times.
- When you answer your own questions it deprives students from constructing and expressing their own thoughts.

6 Instructivism and deep learning

It is, in fact, nothing short of a miracle that the modern methods of instruction have not entirely strangled the holy curiosity of inquiry.
Albert Einstein

In many classrooms, the principle role of the teacher is to deliver subject knowledge, primarily using a lecturing style of teaching, based on a lesson designed around specific curriculum objectives. This form of direct instruction is based on instructivist pedagogy and is focused primarily on content delivery. Within this framework, the teacher's ability to make effective eye contact and use persuasive questioning techniques while structuring the learning environment into manageable chunks of information is crucial. Any trained teacher would recognize this style and lesson format as effective teaching. However, fundamental to this method of teaching, and an often forgotten element when discussing instructivist pedagogy, is the quality of the interaction between the teacher and the student. This form of instruction is teacher–centred and based on behaviourist psychology and, traditionally, educational psychologists have focused on the behaviours of the teacher when discussing effective teaching using this method. The elements of good instruction (and hence good teaching) were first popularized by Robert Gagné in the 1960s and from these principles of effective instruction and traditional methods of teaching developed.

The basic steps of instructivist teaching

Step 1 – The teacher organizes subject content into manageable chunk of information.

Step 2 – Subject content is predetermined and based on specific curriculum objectives.

Step 3 – Subject content is delivered by the teacher and learnt by the student.

Step 4 – Students are assessed on their ability to remember the material.

The Conditions of Learning (Gagné 1965), based on the information processing model, identified the mental conditions needed for effective learning. Largely, Gagné's theory is an instructional theory rather than a learning theory, as a learning theory tends to outline the concepts and processes that are responsible for learning, while an instructional theory describes the conditions under which learning can be achieved (Kruse 2005). However, Gagné's nine-step process, called the 'events of instruction', is a structured process that any teacher would recognize as an effective model for effective classroom teaching. It is not surprising, then, that traditional forms of teaching are seen to be very behaviourist in nature, given that the science of teaching and instruction traditionally was based on this and similar information processing models. Table 6 shows the mental processes associated with each stage of instruction.

Within this framework, the teacher begins by gaining the learner's attention so that they can present the subject content. The goals and objectives of the lesson are presented to the learner to allow them to organize their thoughts. The teacher activates prior learning by reviewing previously learned information and then presents new information by chunking it into manageable portions of knowledge (which reduces information overload). It is crucial during this stage that the information is effectively and strategically sequenced to allow the learner to effectively absorb and retain the information. Guidance and techniques are provided to the learner on how to learn and retain the new information. The learner is given an opportunity

Table 6 Gagné's nine events of instruction and their associated mental processes

Instructional event	Internal mental process
1. Gain attention	Stimuli activates receptors
2. Inform learners of objectives	Creates level of expectation for learning
3. Stimulate recall of prior learning	Retrieval and activation of short-term memory
4. Present the content	Selective perception of content
5. Provide 'learning guidance'	Semantic encoding for storage in long-term memory
6. Elicit performance (practice)	Responds to questions to enhance encoding and verification
7. Provide feedback	Reinforcement and assessment of correct performance
8. Assess performance	Retrieval and reinforcement of content as final evaluation
9. Enhance retention and transfer to the job	Retrieval and generalization of learned skill to new situation

(Taken from Kruse 2005.)

to practice or do something with the new information and specific feedback is given on the learner's performance (i.e. how they can improve). Performance is then assessed (i.e. through questioning or a learning task) and the teacher enhances the retention and transfer of information by reviewing the lesson and showing the learner how the newly learned information transfers to similar problems/contexts.

Model of interaction for instruction

Table 7 outlines a classroom model of interaction based on my experience in an FE classroom, which focuses on the stages of interaction between the teacher and the student. The model outlines a scaffolding process that begins with the teacher

Table 7 Model of interaction for instruction

Stage		
1. Establish the context	Teacher	• Negotiates the learning objectives. • Reflects on previous **and** future topics and how current topic relates.
	Student	• Negotiates learning objectives and presents new topics that they may want covered.

Context: It is important when establishing the context that students are able to have some power to negotiate their learning objectives. This allows them to take some ownership of the learning process and have some 'choice'. It also allows them to point out past topics that they may have had difficulty with which will allow the teacher to weave the topic into the current session.

2. **Presentation** of subject information	Teacher	• Presents the material using multiple examples and demonstrations relating the new information to the students' context and the real world. • Uses questioning techniques to allow students to construct their own understanding. • Fundamental concepts and information are introduced repeatedly in a cyclical process.
	Student	• Reflects on material by seeking meaning and understanding through questions and interaction with the teacher. (Note: the key to this stage of the interaction process is the generation of questions by the student. This can be facilitated by activities that ask students to actively write down questions while the teacher teaches.) • Continually reflects on the information being presented making links between new information and how it relates to existing knowledge and understanding.

Presentation: The presentation stage is meant to confront students' misconceptions, make information meaningful by relating new material to what students already know and understand and promoting transfer and generalizability by making links to the real world and the student context. During the presentation stage, the subject information is introduced in a cyclical process that allows students to gradually build up their knowledge and understanding of the subject. The presentation of the information builds in complexity gradually over the session, allowing students to build their understanding by relating it to their existing knowledge and understanding.

Table 7 *continued*

3. Practice	Teacher/	a) Teacher **demonstrates** the use of the
a) demonstrate	student	new information/skill/knowledge
b) lead		(ISK).
c) demonstrate		b) Teacher **leads** learner through step-
d) extrapolate		by-step using the ISK (x times).
		c) Student then **demonstrates** competence independently by using the ISK (x times).
		d) Student then **extrapolates** past current use of the learned ISK by creating new knowledge (new ways of demonstrating and using ISK).

Practice: The practice stage is a cyclical process of scaffolding practice that sees the teacher gradually relinquishing control of the learning process to the students which allows them to become competent with the new ISK. There are two important elements of this stage: (1) the scaffolding practice and interaction between the teacher and student; and (2) the final stage that allows students to demonstrate new uses and ways of thinking about the ISK. (Note: During this stage teachers can assign a learning activity.) It is important for teachers to confront students' misconceptions, allow students to engage in active learning and make mistakes.

4. **Review** of subject information	Teacher	• Shows how the topic relates to the other topics in the subject/course. • Reviews the new ISK and models problem-solving and critical thinking by using and critically analysing the new ISK. • Uses questioning techniques which encourage students to construct their own understanding of the ISK. • Demonstrates critical thinking skills and extrapolation (thinking about and using the ISK in novel ways).
	Student	• Demonstrates extrapolation and critical thinking using the new ISK. • Queries the teacher on their understanding of the ISK.

Review: During this stage, the teacher reinforces the structure of the curriculum by showing how the new ISK relates to other topics and the course in general. This reinforces the links between the various topics and allows students to begin to construct their own 'universe of knowledge'. The teacher models effective higher-order thinking skills (e.g. analysis, critical thinking).

Table 7 *continued*

5. Provide **feedback** on student performance	Teacher	• Queries and provides feedback on students knowledge and understanding of the new ISK. • Queries students' understanding of the new ISK in relation to the entire course/subject area. • Formal assessment (summative or formative).
	Student	• Interacts with teacher by entering into a dialogue around the new ISK – answering and posing further questions.

Feedback: The feedback stage is ongoing during the entire instructional session. Eventually, at some point in the learning process, there will be some form of formative or summative assessment that uses traditional methods (examinations, essays) of determining whether the new ISK has been learned.

demonstrating and modelling the new information/skills/ knowledge (ISK) and gradually relinquishing control of the learning process to the student. An essential aspect of this model is the high level of interaction between the teacher and the student and the cyclical process by which the information is introduced to the students. Thus, the model does not assume that subject information is introduced in a sequential and hierarchical order. Rather, fundamental concepts and information are introduced repeatedly in a cyclical process. The presentation of the information builds in complexity, also allowing students to develop a more complex understanding of the subject by continually relating it to their existing knowledge and understanding. Further, this model is built on a scaffolding concept that moves the student–teacher interaction through a process that sees the control gradually move from the teacher to the student. Thus, at the beginning of the lesson, the teacher will tend to direct the core of the questions, while at the end of the lesson the students will be responsible for directing the questions. The model is outlined within an instructivist framework, but incorporates both instructivist and constructivist principles.

Important elements of an interaction session that maximizes student engagement

1. Organize the information

The organization of the information is crucial. Every subject has fundamental concepts that need to be learned for students to progress in their understanding of a subject. Therefore, it is essential that these concepts are organized in the appropriate way. Further, this does not mean that the information is ordered sequentially and introduced hierarchically. Rather, it is important for the elements of the subject information to be repeated and re-introduced in a cyclical process whereby students are re-introduced to fundamental concepts in new ways. The information should be introduced so that it builds in complexity, which allows the learner to see how the knowledge is constructed, and how important links between fundamental concepts are built. There is a tendency in FE classrooms to follow the examination subject specifications topic-by-topic, covering a single topic and specific specifications each week so that by the end of the course the teacher can be confident they have covered all the required information and they have completed their job satisfactorily. This is not a pedagogically effective way to structure a course. It is a strategy that has developed because of an environment that is plagued by tight time constraints and extensive examination syllabuses. There needs to be overlap and successive repetition to allow learners multiple perspectives on the same topic. This format allows them to construct their own understanding of a subject. The challenge for the teacher is to do this effectively within the required period (a single year or semester).

2. Highlight important information

The main points of the lesson need to be constantly repeated in a cyclical process. You can always assume a large majority of students did not hear the first four times you repeated the fundamental concepts and essential elements of the lesson. You need to repeat fundamental concepts demonstrating the links between the concepts and other course topics and information constantly and in multiple ways. By continually showing the links between the core subject information, students will begin to understand the complexity of the knowledge domain and cognitively reconstruct this complexity for themselves.

3. Make information meaningful

The subject information needs to be contextual and relate to the students' lives. If they can see how it affects them, it becomes real for them. When it becomes real, it becomes important. When it is important, it is memorable. The most effective way to do this is to relate the subject to students' everyday lives. For example, in an ICT class, relate the Data Protection Act to how your college collects and holds student data or in a biology class talk about how stem cell research may contribute to finding a cure for AIDS and other fatal diseases that affect students and their families.

4. Check and refine students' understanding

This process moves the student–teacher interaction through a cycle that begins with the teacher using effective questioning, to encourage the students to reflect and think critically on the subject. Gradually, the teacher relinquishes control and the students direct the questioning which allows them to seek appropriate information to build their conceptual knowledge and understanding. Encourage students gradually throughout a class session to take control of the learning environment and begin to direct questioning and seek answers for themselves. This allows students to take ownership of their own learning and provides a mechanism for encouraging student's intrinsic motivation for a topic.

5. Promote transfer and generalizability

Assist students in understanding the way that the information they are learning can be transferred to other contexts. This allows students to practise problem-solving and critical thinking by applying a conceptual understanding to practical situations or real-world situations. Developing higher-order thinking skills are essential if students are to become competent citizens who can make their own way in the real world.

Ways of maximizing student engagement

When teachers show a personal interest in the subject that they teach, the enthusiasm is contagious. If you allow students to see your intrinsic interest and excitement about your subject, it encourages them to develop an intrinsic interest.

It is important to show students the structure of the course or subject. You need to show them how each topic relates to the other and how the course or module relates to other courses/modules/disciplines. This allows students to contextualize their learning. Further, fundamental to all subjects are key concepts that students need to understand to become competent within the subject. Ensuring plenty of time is spent on these fundamental concepts allows students to cement these important concepts into their existing knowledge structures. These fundamental concepts become 'enablers' that open up students to new information or ways of thinking in the discipline. Additionally, new information needs to be related to what students already know and understand. Without relating new information to their existing knowledge structures, the subject information becomes bits of unrelated information and fragmented knowledge that is not tied to any fundamental conceptions or understanding.

Further, it is crucial that students are confronted about their fundamental misconceptions of a subject. Often, beginner teachers tend to focus too strongly on the lesson plan and, while very competent with the subject content, do not have the pedagogical understanding to know the common difficulties and misconceptions students often have when learning the subject. They have a 'tunnel view' of their teaching and unexpected student responses that need clarification often go unnoticed or are ignored. To advance and deepen the complexity of their understanding, students need to be confronted about these misconceptions. This allows them to deepen the complexity of their thinking.

Making and correcting mistakes is fundamental to the learning process. Students need to know that they can make mistakes without penalty for failure. They need to know that putting an effort into their thinking and knowledge construction is rewarded and that the active process of learning is more important than the final outcome of that endeavour. Finally, assessment, both formative (ongoing) and summative (final), should incorporate higher-level thinking which asks students to make links between the information and construct their own thoughts. If students know that lower-level thinking like describing and listing facts composes their final assessment, they will approach their studying with these goals in mind. FE students have become very good at playing the assessment game and most have become proficient test-takers. However, as teachers we have the opportunity to provide effective formative assessment throughout the year by providing students with assessment exercises, learning tasks and homework that can encourage them to think critically and engage with the subject.

When we are asked what effective teaching is, we often visualize a teacher standing at the front of a class explaining a concept in a very clear and articulate way, using simple examples and metaphors that easily explain a complex phenomena or concept. As teachers, we need to reflect on how the questions we ask illicit the type of response from students we are trying to achieve. Initially, these questions and the ways that we interact with students in the classroom should be well thought out and planned. With experience, the interaction we have with students and the questions we ask become second nature. We need to encourage students to be active participants in the learning process. The goal is to engage students with what they are learning, in discussions (with both you and their peers) about the ways in which learning tasks can be undertaken and different methods they can approach their studying. We want to model for them ways that they can ask informed and critical questions about accepted theories and viewpoints and develop an awareness of the limited and provisional nature of knowledge in all disciplines.

Strategies and techniques for the classroom

Question generator
Sometimes during a class if the topic is complex and difficult to understand, students feel confused and find that they cannot

verbalize what it is that they do not understand. Thus, they find it difficult to know what questions to ask. Peer questioning provides students with higher-order open-ended questions which allow them to generate a focused discussion in a small group setting. The questions act as generic prompts that students can use to generate specific content-based questions.

1. The teacher gives a brief lecture on a topic.
2. The teacher then provides the students with a list of open-ended questions. These questions are intended to encourage synthesis, comparison and contrast and extrapolation to other contexts. For example:
   How does ... affect ...? Explain why ... Explain how ... What if ...? What do you think causes ...? Why? How does ... relate to what I've learned before? What is the difference between ... and ...? How are ... and ... similar?
3. Using these open-ended questions, students are given five to ten minutes to individually prepare several content-specific questions based on the topic of the lecture just given by the teacher.
4. The students are then put in small groups of three to four and take turns asking their questions and discussing possible answers.
5. At the end, the teacher can collect some of the key questions that were generated in each group and post them on a local intranet site or provide students with a summarized hard copy.

Summary of main points

- When designing a lesson, remember to highlight important information; make information meaningful; leave time to check and refine students' understanding; and promote transfer and generalizability to other subjects, contexts and the real world.
- You need to show personal interest in the subject you are teaching.

- You need to bring out the structure of the subject by showing how the curriculum topics relate to each other.
- You need to concentrate on and ensure plenty of time for key concepts.
- You need to confront students' misconceptions and engage students in active learning.
- You need to relate new material to what students already know and understand.
- Students need to be allowed to make mistakes without fear of a penalty (e.g. poor grade, negative feedback).

Effective teaching should:

- Focus on desired learning outcomes for students, in the form of knowledge, understanding, skill and attitudes.
- Assist students to form broad conceptual understandings while gaining depth of knowledge.
- Encourage the informed and critical questioning of accepted theories and views.
- Develop an awareness of the limited and provisional nature of current knowledge in all fields.
- Show how understanding evolves and is subject to challenge and revision.
- Engage students as active participants in the learning process, while acknowledging that all learning must involve a complex interplay of active learning and knowledge construction and receptive processes.
- Engage students in discussions about ways in which study tasks can be undertaken.
- Respect students' right to express views and opinions.
- Incorporate a concern for the welfare and progress of individual students.
- Proceed from an understanding of students' knowledge, capabilities and backgrounds.
- Encompass a range of perspectives from groups of different ethic backgrounds, socio-economic groups and sex.
- Acknowledge and attempt to meet the demands of students with disabilities.
- Encourage an awareness of the ethical dimensions of problems and issues.

- Utilize instructional strategies and tools to enable many different strategies of learning.
- Adopt assessment methods and tasks appropriate to the desired learning outcomes of the course and topic and to the capabilities of the student.

7 Constructivism and deep learning

What a person thinks on his own without being stimulated by the thoughts and experiences of other people is even in the best case rather paltry and monotonous.

Albert Einstein

Behaviourist theories and information processing theories formed the fundamental tenets of educational theory for decades and it is through these theories that the process–product curriculum with a strong emphasis on didactic instruction emerged. To behaviourists and information processing theorists, learning is simply a matter of storing information for later recall. The typical FE curriculum is based on a structure in which essential subject knowledge has been identified by subject experts and has been converted into a set of behavioural objectives and learning outcomes. The teacher then imparts their complex understanding by breaking these learning outcomes down into manageable chunks of information to be learned by students during various lessons over the course of the academic year.

Much FE teaching is teacher centred and often depends heavily on textbooks to dictate coverage of the course topics. Traditionally, FE teachers have tended to use lecture-style approaches to ensure they have planned their time well and they can get through the syllabus during the course of a year. Further, chief examiners who are very familiar with the examination specifications often write subject textbooks. While these textbooks succinctly cover all the required subject information that tends to show up in final examinations, they imply to students the idea that there is a fixed world of knowledge with right and wrong answers. Thus, students adopt a view that learning is about quantity and to become competent within a subject domain, all they need to do is memorize the information that we present to them (i.e. a quantitative conception of learning).

Teachers are seen as the experts who know all the correct answers and their job is to transfer their knowledge, ideas and understanding to the student. This type of environment, some would argue, leaves little room for student-initiated questions, independent thought or interaction between the students themselves. Over the years, opposition to this educational theory has encouraged support for constructivism (a form of student-centred learning). The central idea of constructivism is that people construct their own knowledge and understanding of a subject through experience. Duckworth (1987) says:

'Meaning is not given to us in our encounters, but it is given by us, constructed by us, each in our own way, according to how our understanding is currently organised' (p. 112).

Students need to find activities in the classroom that are cognitively engaging and relevant to the real world and their own lives. These elements motivate their active participation in the problem-solving process which is critical to the proper facilitation of constructivist learning environments. Learners construct their own knowledge by applying and testing ideas and approaches to new situations based on their current knowledge and experience. Through this process, they are able to integrate the new knowledge gained with their pre-existing cognitive constructs.

Most of us do not have a problem with this idea, as most would agree that our students 'interpret' their experiences in class and then try to make sense of them. The difficulty constructivism poses is its implications for the types of teaching methods teachers have traditionally used in the classroom. An acceptance that constructivist principles are effective methods of teaching would seem to imply that the ways that we have traditionally taught have been inadequate. Accepting that premise would be difficult for any teacher, no matter how progressive their views.

However, many of us have learned through trial and error

some effective means of teaching our subject areas outside of the traditional 'chalk-and-talk' lecture. Regardless of whether we associate these methods of good practice with its theoretical equivalent (constructivism), it is probable that many of us have intermittently used some of these principles throughout our career (e.g. collaborative learning, problem-solving tasks). This is the first step to transforming our practice. Johanssen (1994, p. 35) argues that there are eight characteristics that differentiate constructivist learning environments from the traditional didactic style of teaching. Constructivist learning environments need to:

1. provide multiple representations of information and concepts;
2. represent the complexity of the real world;
3. focus on knowledge construction rather than knowledge reproduction;
4. present authentic learning tasks;
5. provide real-world scenarios rather than planned sequences of instruction;
6. encourage reflection;
7. foster context-dependent knowledge construction;
8. support knowledge construction through social collaboration.

To make constructivist approaches to designing curriculum effective, the learning environment must allow:

- learners to apply current information and knowledge to a problem either individually or in a group to develop new knowledge and understanding;
- learners to assimilate pre-existing views and approaches with new experiences to construct a new level of understanding through trial and error;
- learners to be assessed through performance-based projects or portfolios rather than through traditional methods of short-answer or multiple-choice assessments;
- teachers to see themselves as co-learners and facilitate learning by acting as a support mechanism and stimulating and provoking the learner's critical thinking, analysis and

synthesis throughout the learning process (e.g. through effective questioning).

Scaffolding as a mechanism for facilitating learning

An important element of constructivist theory is *scaffolding*. According to Vygotsky (1978), students' skills fall into three categories:

1. Skills which the student cannot perform.
2. Skills which the student may be able to perform.
3. Skills which the student can perform with help.

The purpose of scaffolding is to assist the learner to reach their 'zone of proximal development' (ZPD) which Vygotsky defines as:

> The distance between a child's actual developmental level as determined by independent problem-solving and the higher level of potential development as determined through problem-solving under adult guidance or in collaboration with more capable peers (p. 86).

Scaffolding is a process whereby a teacher or peer provides an appropriate level of assistance to a learner which allows them to work at a higher level than they would otherwise be able to. Scaffolding allows students to perform tasks that would normally be slightly beyond their ability. Thus, appropriate teacher facilitation can allow students to function at the cutting edge of their individual development.

Strategies and techniques for the classroom

Interactive constructivist-based (individual or group) tasks can enhance the learning that takes place in the classroom. Students need to be able to seek out information, experiment with information/knowledge and actively use subject information. They need to collect and analyse data, employ problem-solving strategies, actively observe phenomena they are studying and conduct experiments. They need the opportunity to select appropriate resources for their learning tasks and design models (physically and conceptually) to explain and demonstrate their understanding. These active learning processes can be done in both individual and group work.

The following section provides some useful generic techniques that, with a little imagination, can be adapted to any subject or course in further education. These techniques can be changed and adapted to particular subjects and contexts. The key element is the active cognitive engagement of the students with the learning tasks.

Small group activities
(Adapted for the FE classroom from Ginnis 2002)

Collaborative answers
This group activity involves students working together in small groups of three to four to develop answers to questions posed by the teacher. The collaboration process encourages students to negotiate with other members of the group and reach a consensus for an answer. The key to this group exercise is that the questions posed to the groups are tied closely to the examination specifications for each topic and the questions require high-level thinking (reflecting, hypothesizing, etc.).

Each group is assigned a team name and each group member is assigned a number. You pose a question to the students who examine the possibilities and construct an answer. You pick the team by drawing their team name from a hat and rolling a dice to choose a group member who will answer the question. Then you draw another team. Each team has a chance to answer each question. Alternatively, you could break the groups into even teams and have two teams 'show down' for each question while the other groups choose the group that has given the best answer. A round is complete when each group has taken part in a show down with another team.

The activity encourages learners to construct their own knowledge by integrating course information with personal experience and their current knowledge. Further, the activity encourages each learner to engage individually with subject information because any group member could be called in any round to answer the question.

Debate

Divide the class in half, instead of groups of three or four. The groups should then divide themselves into defence and prosecution sub-teams. Then:

1. Give each half of the class a different cause to support that links the learning goal and the text/object/concept.
2. Give them time to prepare evidence to support their case.
3. The first group presents their case.
4. The second group's prosecution team then cross-examines the first group.
5. The first group defence team responds.
6. Repeat these three steps with the other half of the class.
7. You (as judge) decide which case is more persuasive and why; but be sure to acknowledge the strengths of both sides!

Perspectives – group problem-solving

1. Find a compelling problem concerning a course topic/concept.
2. As a class, choose several different perspectives from which to approach the problem.
3. Assign each group a different perspective.
4. Give them time to solve the problem.
5. Each group takes turns presenting their solutions.
6. After each group presents, the other groups should be given a few minutes to question/challenge/debate with the group.
7. Combining the perspectives – close the exercise by finding the connections between each of the solutions, showing how they complete each other. This can be done in the small groups or as a class. Find the ideal solution to the problem, combining all the perspectives.

The jigsaw
This group activity works with any complex problem that can be broken down into four to five components.

1. Assign each group an area in which to develop expertise.
2. Give the groups time to analyse the text/object/concept in depth from their respective angles of expertise.
3. Re-shuffle the groups so that there is one member from each of the original groups in each new group.
4. Now have each group solve a problem concerning the text/object/concept with their four experts weighing in with each angle of analysis.
5. Have each group present their results and discuss the differences.

Individual activities

Mind mapping
Of central importance to constructivist theory is that learning must be student-centred. Mind mapping is a good method for helping a learner to create a visual representation of their current understanding of a subject or course. This allows learners to reflect on, develop and organize their thoughts and understanding about a subject. It also demonstrates to students how different topics relate to each other.

Argument writing
This technique involves presenting students with multiple sources of information on a specific curriculum topic area and instructing them to write an argument from a certain position (which is decided by the teacher) and providing evidence for their argument from the source documents. The technique is effective when the sources are real-world documents (i.e. magazine articles, policy documents) because the students can relate this information to the real world.

Argument writing – AS ICT

In an AS level ICT class, students were given copies of computer magazine articles, websites and government reports on the possible effects of the electromagnetic radiation that is given off by mobile phones. One half of the class was asked to write an argument to support the funding of government research into the ill effects of mobile phones and their connection to cancer, while providing solid support from the documents. Similarly, the other half of the class was asked to write an argument that the research should not be supported and that there is no supportive research evidence for the negative effects of mobile phones. This task allowed the students to engage with multiple source documents that provided evidence for both sides of an argument. The completed task was then used as a starting point for a class debate.

AS ICT – The social aspect of ICT
AQA Specification 10.5

Summary of main points

When teaching using a constructivist framework a consideration of the following elements is important:

- A variety of representations and multiple perspectives are needed.
- The teacher acts as guide and facilitator rather than the expert.
- The learning environment, activities and assessment should encourage problem solving, critical thinking and reflection.
- The student needs to take ownership of the learning process.
- Learning tasks need to be context based and represent the complexities of the 'real world'.
- Knowledge construction rather than reproduction should be emphasized in the classroom, learning activities and assessment.

- Higher-order thinking skills should be emphasized in the classroom, learning activities and assessment.
- Students are encouraged to seek knowledge independently.
- Peer collaboration allows students to work with and learn from each other.
- Scaffolding is a useful tool that assists students in performing beyond the limits of their ability.
- Assessment should be formative and ongoing to allow students to advance their knowledge and understanding.

8 Problem-based learning in the FE classroom

Problems cannot be solved at the same level of awareness that created them.

Albert Einstein

Problem-based learning (PBL) has been used as a pedagogical tool in many professional fields including medicine, business, social work, management and engineering (Boud and Feletti 1997) and the current popularity of PBL in today's classroom has spawned many variations (Barrows 2000). Using PBL with FE students allows teachers to guide students through the problem-solving process and allows students to use higher-order thinking skills in an active learning environment while investigating topics based on examination subject specifications. PBL incorporates many constructivist principles of learning and curriculum design and allows teachers to create problem situations for students in which they can explore a topic and collect the needed information to solve a given problem. The key element for FE teachers is using the examination subject specifications to develop the problem situations. This aligns the PBL task directly to the course learning outcomes.

What is PBL?

PBL focuses on the process of learning rather than on acquiring substantive subject knowledge and Barrows (2003) outlines the important elements of PBL that teachers need to consider when they plan classroom activities using this approach. While Barrows focuses strongly on an ill-structured environment, realistically, for teachers under tight time constraints and a structured curriculum, a well-defined or moderately well-defined problem are the most practical for PBL learning tasks in further education. This allows the teacher to gauge their time and design a focused task that is structured around the examination specifications. For a problem to be well defined, there must be one clearly preferable solution.

A 'moderately well-defined' problem has more than one acceptable solution, whereas an ill-defined problem may potentially have no solution. Often using subject-specific case-based examples is an effective way to structure a 'well-defined' problem. The discussion of a case study serves to encourage students to activate relevant prior knowledge and it stimulates students' interest and thus their intrinsic motivation to learn the subject. Finally, it sets a context for learning similar to one in which students may find themselves in the future (Schmidt and Moust 2000).

The following PBL process (Barrows 2003) has been adapted to the FE context for courses that are based on a national curriculum. Within the FE classroom, the information and understanding expected of students is outlined in the examination board subject specifications and the PBL activity should be flexible, yet streamlined to curriculum subject specifications (to focus student learning). Materials from the course can be used to focus the student's investigation, with an emphasis on using outside materials that allow students to move past the confines of the curriculum. While this streamlines the learning to some degree, there needs to be an equilibrium, which is maintained by the teacher, between a focus on the curriculum objectives and the flexibility for students to explore outside the curriculum. This allows students to guide their own learning and to link course and subject information to new knowledge that has been acquired through self-directed investigation.

Problem-based learning essentials for the FE classroom

- Students must take ownership and responsibility for their own learning.
- Collaboration with peers is essential. Each student must have individual responsibility for a specific task and the completion of this task is fundamental for the completion of the PBL activity.
- Learning should be integrated in and combine with a wide range of topics within the curriculum.
- The learning outcomes and objectives of the PBL activity must be explicitly tied to the learning outcomes outlined in the examination specifications. Teacher facilitation and questioning must focus learning on these learning outcomes.
- The case study used in the PBL task must allow students to investigate the problem from multiple perspectives and course topics and also allow them the flexibility for free enquiry from topics outside the curriculum.
- What students learn during their self-directed enquiry must be applied back to the case study or problem under investigation.
- The opportunity for students to present their conclusions and demonstrate what they have learned while making reference to course concepts and principles is essential.
- The PBL activity must simulate a real-world activity.

(Adapted from Barrows (2003))

To create an effective PBL task takes time and careful planning. You need to prepare the proper materials, design a structured task based on curriculum subject specifications and strategically facilitate students through guidance and questioning to focus their learning on the subject specifications. If this is done well, Stepien (1999b) argues students will be able to:

1. *Engage* – investigate a real world problem while engaging with subject information.
2. *Inquire and investigate* – seek out relevant information through a variety of resources including course text-books, the Internet, library resources, etc.
3. *Evaluate and justify* – interpret new information and develop solutions and applications for a real world problem.
4. *Communicate* – demonstrate new knowledge to teachers (i.e. report), peers (i.e. class presentation) or the world (i.e. webpage).

Facilitating PBL – the role of the teacher

Wolff (2000) believes that teachers can stimulate interest in the learning activity and the problems they present to students by showing their own interest in the problem, by modelling the problem-solving process that they want their students to use and by using effective questioning to encourage critical thinking. For example, using probing (e.g. What do you mean?) or reflection questions (e.g. How does this idea help you?) encourages students to meta-reflect. Further, teachers can encourage collaboration between group members by asking involvement questions (e.g. Who else has ideas on this?) Finally, it is the teacher's responsibility to increase or decrease the challenge when there are signs of boredom or confusion. A teacher's use of probing questions when facilitating inquiry into problems is an essential component of PBL. Paul (1993) argues that the strategic use of questioning is meant to help learners arrive at judgements that are based on their own reasoning. He outlines a taxonomy of Socratic questions that build upon each other but are not confined to a sequenced pattern. The role of the teacher in a PBL environment is to keep the inquiry focused on the problem, but to allow students to arrive at conclusions based on their own critical analysis and reasoning. Table 8 has been adapted from Stepien (1999a) and gives some examples of Socratic questions that can be used to facilitate PBL activities.

Table 8 Socratic questioning to facilitate PBL activities

Questions of clarification

'What do you mean by . . .?', 'What is your main point?', 'How does . . . relate to . . .?', 'Could you put that another way?', 'What do you think is the main issue here?', 'How does this relate to our problem/discussion/ issue?', 'What do you take . . . to mean by his remark?', 'Can you summarize in your own words what . . . said?'

Questions that probe assumptions

'What are you assuming?', 'What is . . . assuming?', 'What could we assume instead?', 'You seem to be assuming . . . do I understand you correctly?', 'All of your reasoning depends on the idea that . . . is this correct?', 'Why have you based your reasoning on . . . instead of . . .?', 'Is that always the case?', 'Why would someone make that assumption?'

Questions that probe reasons and evidence

'What would be an example?', 'Why do you think that is true?', 'Do you have any evidence for that?', 'What are your reasons for saying that?', 'What other information do you need?', 'Are these reasons adequate?', 'How does that apply to this case?', 'Is there a reason to doubt that evidence?', 'Can someone else provide evidence to support that view?', 'What reasoning brought you to that conclusion?'

Questions about viewpoints or perspectives

'What are you implying by that?', 'But, if that happened, what else would happen as a result?', 'Why?', 'What effect would that have?' 'What would be an alternative?' If . . . and . . . is the case, then what might also be true?'

Questions that probe implications and consequences

'How can we find out?', 'What does this question assume?', 'To answer this question, what other questions must we answer first?', 'I'm not sure I understand how you are interpreting this question. Is this the same as . .?' 'Why is this issue important?' 'Is this the most important question, or is there an underlying question that is really the issue?'

(Taken from Stepien (1999b) 'Tutorial on problem-based learning', which was originally adapted from R. Paul (1993) *Critical Thinking: How to Prepare Students for a Rapidly Changing World.*)

Wolff (2000) argues that if students are to effectively engage in problem-based learning they need to:

1. Explore the problem – clarify terms and concepts that are not understandable, create hypotheses, identify issues.
2. Identify what they know initially that is important to the problem.
3. Identify what they need to know.
4. As a group, prioritize the learning tasks so that each group member has an equal role and allocate resources.
5. Search for information needed to solve the problem and the particular task they have been assigned.
6. Return to the group; share their new knowledge with the entire group which will allow the other members of the group to assimilate the information with what they have learnt.
7. As a group, apply the information and knowledge to the problem and attempt to integrate the knowledge acquired into a comprehensive explanation.
8. Demonstrate and present their learning – possibly in a presentation to the teacher, rest of the class, webpage, etc.

PBL curriculum design considerations for FE teachers

Questions teachers should ask themselves:

- Will the case study generate critical discussion and present learning opportunities that are relevant to the examination specifications for the subject?
- Does the case provide an adequate level of challenge and encourage the use of skills that would be required of students working at their specific level (e.g. critical thinking, research skills)?
- Does the case sufficiently integrate different topics from within the course?
- Does the case contain a sufficient description and context that will focus students' exploration but leave enough flexibility to not confine their learning opportunities?

- Is the case example relevant to the student's situation? Will the case be interesting and motivate students to engage in the activity?
- Is the case study realistic/authentic?
- Can the PBL learning task be completed in the time available?

The PBL process

Teachers present students with a case study and students work in groups to analyse the problem, research, discuss and produce tentative explanations, solutions or recommendations. It is essential to the PBL process that students do not have sufficient prior knowledge to address the problem. If they do, the process of critical reflection is lost. In the initial discussion, students develop a set of questions/task statements that need to be addressed. These questions then become the objectives for students' learning. It is important at this point that the teacher facilitates the setting of the objectives in line with the examination specifications.

1. *Present the case study and problem statement* – The case study takes a real-world issue (possibly something that has recently been in the news) that is robust enough to cover many of the curriculum topics and is closely tied to the subject examination specifications (see case example below).

2. *Students list what they know, what they do not know and what they need to know* – This may include data from the case study and information based on prior knowledge that they may have gained during earlier lessons.

3. *List what is needed to solve the problem* – Teams develop a research plan to study their problem. Students will need to find information to fill in things they do not know. They will also list questions to guide their searches that may take place online, in the library and using other media of investigation.

4. *List recommendations, solutions or hypotheses and carry out possible actions* – Students formulate and test solutions to

the case-study problem. They critically evaluate the information collected from group members and combine it into a coherent whole. They analyse the feasibility of the individual solutions and investigate practical applications of the information to the problem.

5. *Present and support their findings* – Students will present their findings to the teacher or the rest of the class. This can be done both orally and/or in writing. The report should include the problem, questions generated by the group, the information gathered, the data analysis and the recommendations or solution that the group generated. Often, at this point, it is useful for students from different groups to engage in a critical discussion of the best solution to the case problem.

Computing/IT PBL case example: Data Protection Act
Using PBL learning tasks in computing/IT to introduce topics to students allows them to put the information into a real-world context and understand how ICT impacts on people in everyday life. For example, by presenting students with a real-world scenario (e.g. data protection case studies) teachers can ask students to apply their course material (e.g. data protection legislation) to the PBL case study. This allows students to see the real-world application of the course material and actively apply the subject information to a real-world context. The AQA 10.9 subject specification for ICT (the legal framework) states that students should be able to:

- recall the rights of individuals under the legislation;
- recall the nature, purpose and provisions of the current data protection legislation of the Public Register;
- explain how the requirements of the legislation impact on data collection and use;
- describe the obligations of data users under the legislation;
- recall the rights of individuals under the legislation.

The following case example was presented to the students in an AS ICT class and in collaborative groups students were asked to make a decision on the case example using their knowledge and understanding of the Data Protection Act.

Case example – problem-based learning activity

Data Protection Act

Students in an AS ICT class were studying the Data Protection Act and the legal issues that have arisen with the
advent of ICT into society. The excerpt below was taken
from the Information Commissioner's Office website
(www.informationcommissioner.gov.uk) and describes a
case that came to their attention. Students were arranged in
groups and given the case study without the Information
Commissioner's final decision on the case. The students
worked through the case example detailing what they
knew and what they needed to know. They discussed and
evaluated possible solutions/conclusions supported by the
course material and other sources (e.g. copies of the Data
Protection Act, the Internet) to deal with the case example. The purpose of the activity was to allow them to apply
their understanding of the Data Protection Act. When the
groups had agreed on a course of action they were given
the opportunity to relay this solution back to the rest of the
class. The actual decision reached by the Commissioner
was then given to the students and discussed in relation to
the conclusions/decisions that students had come to in
their small groups.

Note: The solution that the students arrive at is not as
important as how they arrive at a decision and the evidence
that they provide to support their reasoning.

International bank – the recording of telephone calls

I received a complaint from an individual who stated that
in the course of her employment for a particular company
she received a telephone call from one of the major
international banking organizations based in Ireland. In the
course of the call, she heard 'pips' on the line and, on
enquiring, was informed that the call was being recorded
but no explanation for the recording was given by the
person representing the bank.

My Office contacted the banking organization involved and inquired why people were not made aware that the calls were being recorded. It clearly is important in data protection terms that an individual is aware of and gives consent to such recordings. I, of course, appreciate that in the financial world it can be necessary when telephone instructions are given that some record has to be available in case a dispute arises.

In response, the bank stated that, in line with industry practice in the financial services sector in Ireland, it operated an automated telephone recording system. Under this system, calls are automatically recorded and the recordings are retained for one year. Access to these recordings, permitted only under strictly controlled conditions, is limited either to where evidence is required in the case of a dispute by a customer as to an instruction or confirmation given, or where there is an investigation of suspected fraud or other criminal activity. Only a limited number of senior individuals had access to the recordings, which are kept in a secure room in a secure locked cabinet and then only where documentation had been completed and approved.

The bank initially disputed whether personal data was involved, arguing that although the system was capable of automatic operation in that it listed details of particular calls made at a particular time, to or from a particular telephone number, it was questionable whether the recordings contain data relating to an 'identifiable individual'.

The bank also indicated that their target market in Ireland is aimed at a strict market consisting of multinational corporates, financial institutions and the Government, and that their business in Ireland was not retail based. It stated that the telephone recording system which they operated at the time of the Office's enquiry was first implemented in 2000 and did not have the capability of restricting the recording of calls to specific telephone extensions or business critical areas. It was in the process of installing a new system which would have the capability to limit the recording of calls to business-critical areas only. It was also

> introducing automated messages within the telephone system which would advise that the call was being recorded and the purpose of the recording.
>
> AS ICT – The legal framework
> AQA Specification 10.9

Potential pitfalls when using PBL

Stepien (1999a) outlines the potential problems when using a PBL approach. The following section adapts these pitfalls to the FE context.

Students

- For most students in FE, using alternative forms of teaching in the classroom will be a culture shock. They are not used to these methods and it may confuse and frustrate them. Students will assume if you are not standing at the front of the class and lecturing them, like so many of their teachers before you, you are not doing your job as a teacher. However, the more you use these forms of teaching, the easier it will be for students and they will eventually see the benefits of these techniques in their own understanding of the subjects they are learning.
- Students will want the information they need to absorb to get a good grade in the subject. They will associate success with the quantity of information that they can consume and remember for test purposes. Giving them a copy of a grading rubric will help them to understand the assessment process for these activities and should help them to understand what is expected of them. The key point is that the rubric reflects higher-level learning outcomes (e.g. critical thinking, analysis) as well as lower-level learning outcomes (e.g. describe, list).
- Small group work, if used effectively, will allow students to contribute to and take an active role in their learning. However, if group work is not monitored and supported effectively by the teacher, individual members can easily

fall by the wayside. Students must learn to take an active role in the group work.

- Students must take 'ownership' of their own learning. They need to be self-directed in seeking knowledge and information to solve group work problems rather than expecting the teacher to do it for them.

Teachers

- Teachers will need to become accustomed to encouraging students to reflect on their own learning by using effective questioning techniques.
- Materials need to be carefully prepared and to provide adequate resources that meet the requirements of the PBL task.
- The problems must be relevant to the course and the student's context. Students need to understand how the problem affects their lives.
- Adequate classroom time needs to be set aside, as PBL can be time consuming. Rushing the PBL process will affect the level of engagement students have with the task.
- Students need to engage critically to a substantive depth so teachers must avoid oversimplifying the problem and offering too much advice to students.

Summary of main points

- Students need to demonstrate critical thinking by applying their course information to real-world situations.
- PBL provides a powerful way of enhancing learning in the classroom by involving students in motivating and challenging problems that prompt reflection and deep approaches to learning.
- PBL places students in real-world scenarios which show students that what they are learning affects their everyday lives.
- PBL uses learning activities that encourage the development of understanding and assesses learning in ways which demonstrate understanding rather than rote learning.

- PBL develops students' collaboration, communication and problem-solving skills.
- PBL promotes higher-order thinking by encouraging students to be critical, reflective and creative thinkers.
- Teachers need to facilitate learning by using probing questions and reflective questions.

9 General techniques to engage learners

It is the supreme art of the teacher to awaken joy in creative expression and knowledge.

Albert Einstein

Engaging students at a deeper level encourages the use of higher-order thinking skills (e.g. problem solving, critical thinking) and improves their understanding of the subject. Wiley and Voss (1999) found that the students who wrote arguments gained a better understanding of the subject matter than those students who wrote narratives or simple descriptions. De Grave *et al.* (2001) found that a deeper interaction with the information promotes better retention and encourages students to use the information to construct meaning that is personally relevant to them. It is this constructive activity and deeper engagement, the researchers concluded, that is correlated with better understanding. Therefore, we need to need to design learning activities for our students that encourage them to engage with the subject information on a deeper level.

These studies suggest that students benefit most from contexts that require deeper interaction with the information which allow them the opportunity to construct their own knowledge. Tasks that can be performed with a more superficial interaction do not necessarily lead to understanding. Furthermore, these findings emphasize the idea that conditions that promote retention of information are not necessarily the same contexts that promote better understanding. The research suggests that deeper engagement gives students the ability to demonstrate their understanding of material (Whelan 1988; Balla *et al.*, 1990; Trigwell and Sleet 1990); develop their conceptions of material (Van Rossum and Schenk 1984; Prosser and Millar 1989) and achieve higher grades (Entwistle and Ramsden 1983; Ramsden et al. 1986; Eley 1992; Drew and Watkins 1998). However, the type of assessment (e.g. multiple-choice versus essay question) has a major impact on the way that students engage with a learning task. Unfortunately, the majority of FE courses are assessed by year-end examinations that are composed largely of short-answer questions. Further, where the questions ask for longer answers, they are often worded in a way that elicits lower-order thinking skills (e.g. questions that ask students to list, describe or identify).

Lizzio et al. (2002) found that the relationship between study approaches and grades may be moderated by the extent to which the assessment used to measure students' achievement emphasizes understanding or reproduction of knowledge. Wiley and Voss (1999) point out multiple-choice and short-answer tests that stress the recall of facts without requiring deeper thought may actually be biased against students who engage in deeper processing. Scouller (1998) noted that multiple-choice and short-answer tests induce surface approaches to studying, while essay and problem-based tests encourage deep approaches to studying. This is troubling considering the high percentage of short-answer questions in many FE examinations.

Creating classrooms that maximize student engagement

Students bring to the classroom a range of prior experiences, varying levels of abilities, prior knowledge and understanding and differing motives and expectations about teaching and learning. These factors affect their expectations of their role as a student and their willingness to take responsibility for their own learning and engage with a course. Too often in the classroom, it becomes evident that students expect teachers to do the work for them by telling them exactly what they need to study and how to answer the examination questions.

Lizzio et al. (2002) found that the two strongest predictors of the development of higher-order competencies, while a complex process, were a teaching environment conducive to learning and opportunities for independence and choice in subject content and process. This supports the argument that independent learning processes (enhancing student perceptions of relevance and ownership), in combination with a positive motivational context derived from environment-enhancing intrinsic motivation, are the dual elements central to the facilitation of effective higher-order learning outcomes (Trigwell and Prosser 1991a; Ramsden 1992). For us as teachers, this means that by encouraging the intrinsic interest our students may have in a subject and giving them some choice about how they learn, teachers will encourage them to engage with a course. The following sections present a few techniques and strategies for maximizing student engagement in the classroom.

Intrinsic motivators
In my previous study (Weyers 2005), I found that if students can approach the course from a perspective that interests them, they find it easier to learn the course material. Thus, as teachers we can encourage students to develop an *intrinsic motivator*, or rather, an intrinsic interest in one area of the curriculum. This interest can be used as a foundation to relate other course information to, and can be used as a motivator that guides a student's enquiry. Intrinsic motivators act as 'knowledge anchors'. When students have a particular interest or motivation for a specific topic within a subject, they can use it as an 'anchor' to which they can link other course information that is less interesting to them. For example, if a student has a keen interest in networking, then they can use that intrinsic interest to engage other course information and try to determine how 'networking' relates to the other course topics (e.g. security).

Cognitive conflict – tasks to encourage learning
This technique involves asking the students to seek out information and construct an argument for a certain position when the source documents only provide evidence 'against' the position you have asked them to take. This mental conflict engages students because it encourages them to seek deeper into the meaning of the facts presented to them, as they cannot find information to support their position. Although they will not construct convincing arguments, the depth of engagement will

allow the students to remember the information they are engaging with – which is the point of the exercise. Following the task, you can have a class discussion based on an alternate argument that the text information does support.

Integrating lesson design models

It is impractical to think that you could use a single style of teaching throughout a school year. Different methods are used at different times, depending on the topic, method of assessment, time restraints, etc. You will find it useful, however, to develop a template structure that you work within when you plan your lessons. This will allow you to plan thought-provoking and motivating lessons strategically and more efficiently and will reduce your workload because you do not need to reinvent the wheel constantly. However, the template structure that you use will be completely dependent on your own preferences and what works for your students. The following templates present some examples of combinations of models that may be useful. (Please note: the interactionist model was introduced in Chapter 6 as an adaptation of the instructivist method of teaching.)

Instructivist/constructivist lesson model

Below is a lesson outline for a 100-minute double lesson (two 50-minute lessons).

Time (minutes)	Topic	Activity
10	Overview of subtopic 1	Mini-lecture
15–20	Use subtopic 1 in a task	Constructivist learning task – student group work
10	Overview of subtopic 2	Mini-lecture
15–20	Use subtopic 2 in a task	Constructivist learning task – student group work
5–10	Break	

10	Overview of subtopics 1 and 2	Mini-lecture
30	Use subtopics 1 and 2 in a task	Constructivist learning task – group work
10	Overview of lesson and learning outcomes	Class discussion/ conclusion by teacher

The important elements of this design are:

1. Try not to talk at students for more than 10 minutes at a time.
2. The learning tasks need to build upon each other so that the last task is a combination that covers the subtopics and allows students to combine all the elements that have been covered in the lesson.

PBL model lesson

This is a lesson outline for a 100-minute double lesson (two 50-minute lessons).

Time (minutes)	Topic	Activity
5		Task instructions
50	All subtopics	PBL learning task – group work
10	Break	
20		Presentation of results/solutions by small groups
10	All topics	Mini-lecture – overview and discussion of proposed solutions

The important elements of this design are:

1. The main focus of this lesson is on the PBL activity. Therefore, this type of lesson should be done at the very start of the introduction of a topic or after the completion of a topic of study. It can be used as a way of wrapping together all the topic information and applying it to a real-world scenario in a practical way or it can be used as an introduction to a topic as a reference point for

discussion when the topics are covered in the following weeks.

2. The final mini-lecture clarifies the main points of the topic that the teacher feels are important and were not covered as effectively as they could have been. It is also a time to have students reflect on what they have learned during the PBL activity and how it applies to their context/life.

Lesson design – key points to remember

1. *Student attention span* – Students find it difficult to concentrate in a classroom when teachers talk for more than 15–20 minutes. Therefore, any mini-lectures that are done during a teaching session should be restricted to approximately 15 minutes. In these situations, it is useful to split up the amount of time you lecture to the class with in-class activities and small group discussions. Further, each mini-lecture should focus on specific curriculum specifications and be followed by a constructivist or PBL learning task to reinforce the information.

2. *Linking curriculum objectives* – All lectures, presentations and learning tasks should make explicit the curriculum specification being covered so that students understand what it is and why they are learning the topic. Further, links between the various subject specifications need to be made so that students see that the examination specifications are not a mass of unrelated facts/information but are actually part of a coherent whole subject.

3. *Learning tasks to link subject information* – Constructivist or PBL learning tasks are effective mechanisms for developing higher-order subject knowledge and understanding. When you have come to the end of a unit or topic, learning tasks can be developed that incorporate the topic specifications into a single learning task. The task problem is developed from the subject specifications and asks the students to engage in an activity that 'uses' the subject information to create, construct, extrapolate or hypothesize from the subject information. This allows

the students to use the information to construct their own meaning and understanding of a topic.

Strategies and techniques for the classroom
(Adapted for the FE classroom from Ginnis 2002)

Correct the teacher
This technique critically engages students in the classroom. It encourages them to attend to what you are saying and to the accuracy of the information that you are conveying to them.

1. This technique creates an environment within the classroom that encourages students to point out and catch all the incorrect and inconsistent things that you may say about a topic or subject.
2. Have them create a list during a class. Alternatively, you could have them point out the incorrect information as you progress through the class. This could be a useful tool for encouraging class participation.
3. This technique encourages students to not only attend to what you are saying but also cognitively engage with the information you are covering to be able to point out any incorrect or inconsistent things that you may have said.
4. At the end of the class, you will want to discuss the inconsistencies that were missed by the students during the class. You may want to keep a score board during the year for individuals or teams. Students will enjoy being able to point out incorrect things that you have said and it will become somewhat of a game.

Application
English language teachers can use it to have students point out mistakes in pronunciation or syntax. *Science* based teachers (biology, physics, chemistry) can use incorrect technical terminology, miscalculate formulas or do an experiment incorrectly, while *computing and IT* teachers can use inconsistent programming syntax and incorrect technical terminology.

Information puzzle

Each student in the class is given a crucial piece of information (on a card or piece of paper) about a topic that is being covered in class and the task is to put the information puzzle together.

1. Explain to the class that each student has an important piece of information. With a large class, it is useful to have more than one task. For example, you may want to provide instructions for an experiment that the students must carry out, a task that is to be completed or a problem that is to be solved, etc.
2. Explain the ground rules that dictate how the students will work together. To work on communication or organizational skills you may want to restrict them from speaking to each other or from looking at their own piece of information until they have found their working groups.
3. Once students have determined their groups, rules for completing the task need to be set. For example, to carry out the task, experiment, etc., only one person can write, only one person can talk, and so forth.
4. Adjust the rules to the type of task that students are being asked to perform. The rules that are created should challenge the students' ability to organize and solve problems. Overcoming these obstacles is part of the learning process.

Applications

In *computing* students can be given the syntax or pseudo code for a small program and be asked to put the program together. In *science*, students can be given the clues needed to solve a particular problem. In *English literature*, students can be given parts of a plot sequence for a play and they have to construct the play.

Modelling

Using simple materials that you can find at home (e.g. string, toilet paper rolls, straws) students can create model replicas of concept, process or technology. For example, computing/IT students could use these materials to simulate a client–server–

based network or biology students could model the circulatory system of the human body. Often, the task can be set in a problem-based format that requires students to solve a problem and create a model to demonstrate their solution.

1. Arrange the students in groups of three or four. Separate the resources into boxes and give a box to each small group.
2. The students are then given a task (e.g. create a client-server network) and asked to create a model of a real-world object.
3. Students can label the pieces of the model that correspond to the real-life object (e.g. computer server, printer, coaxial cable).
4. After the models have been created, students should have the opportunity to share their creations. Students can present their model to the teacher and the rest of the class. Students then have the chance to query groups about aspects of their design. Fundamental elements of the model that have been omitted are a good starting point for a class discussion.

Application
Any real-life object can be modelled. In *computing/IT*, students can create models of the insides of a computer, a topology of a computer network, etc. In *science*, students can create the elements of the periodic table, and *history* students can create models of historical landscapes or ancient civilizations.

Case example – modelling a network topology

Computer network analysts: creating a network topology

Students were arranged into groups of four and told that they were network specialists. They were given a scenario in which they had to design a network (i.e. topology, communication links, hardware and software needed) for a high-street business that wanted to install a network and communicate with its sister company across London.

The students chose names for the companies, broke the job into separate tasks and they engaged in the task by attempting to choose the relevant network solution for the given scenario. They were all responsible for an element of the task. They then took turns presenting their proposal to the group (one group at a time) with each team member being responsible for presenting a certain part of the proposal. The students had the opportunity to query each group on their rationale for aspects of their proposal. This allowed students to use what they had learned to formulate further questions, reflect, and apply that understanding. At the end of the presentations, the teacher chose the proposal that best fitted the solution to the problem scenario and explained the choice. The class then discussed the decision and had the opportunity to provide counter evidence to support their proposals.

AS ICT – Network Environments
AQA ICT subject specification 10.9

Learning teams

Learning teams allow students to engage with a topic and teach it to their peers. This allows students to take ownership and responsibility for their own learning. Additionally, learning information to teach it to someone else demands much more cognitive engagement than simply learning something to remember it.

1. Students are arranged in groups of three or four. Each student within the group is responsible for learning an aspect of the topic that is being presented in the class.
2. Each group is a learning team. The teacher assigns four or five subtopics and each group member is responsible to learn their subtopic.
3. Each group decides which team member to assign to learn each subtopic and then the teacher gives the class a set amount of time to investigate and learn the topic and report to their team.
4. The teacher prepares set material on each subtopic and

provides some guidance on other places the information can be found (e.g. the Internet, library).

5. When the students separate to investigate their subtopic, the students investigating similar subtopics can help each other to create notes, learn the information and plan how they will present it to the rest of their team when they return to their groups.

6. When the set time has elapsed, the students return to their teams to teach the rest of their group the subtopic.

7. Students discuss how the information that their peers have learned relates to the topic they have learned.

Application
This can be applied to various topics in all subject areas as long as a single topic can be divided into four or five subtopics.

Implications for the classroom

Below is a brief synopsis of the key factors that teachers must take into consideration when teaching to maximize student engagement (adapted from the Enhancing Education @ Carnegie Mellon website (2002)):

1. Highlight important information

- *Use clear cues to get students' attention*:
  - ○ point out key information that students need to be aware of and show how it relates to other topics and subjects and the real world;
  - ○ when pointing out things that will be covered in the examination use phrases such as 'In the exam, everyone should be able to . . .'.
- *Provide students with different ways of interacting with the subject information*:
  - ○ give students a variety of learning activities (PBL tasks, group work tasks, mini-lectures with critical discussion);
  - ○ use effective questioning that encourages students to actively and critically engage during the lesson.

- *Allow students to check their own understanding*:
  - use the time at the end of the lesson to summarize the most important points and allow students to reflect on their own learning;
  - tell students directly what they are expected to be able to do with the course material in assignments or exams.

2. Make information meaningful

- *Explain new material in relation to students' prior knowledge* (or possible misconceptions) as prior knowledge can act as an anchor for new knowledge.
- *Relate the subject information to the real world and the students' context.*
- *Ask questions that require higher-order thinking skills (critical analysis, problem solving, reflecting)* to assist students to develop more complex thinking skills.
- *Show relevance* to students' long-term professional goals and/or personal interests.

3. Organize information

- *Use repetition* of concepts and information to allow students to continually construct their understanding by revisiting information to decide where the new and old information fits within their current understanding.
- *Encourage students to take a holistic view* of the course by pointing out how each concept or topic is related to the other modules and the course in general.

4. Check and refine students' understanding

- *Ask a variety of simple and complex questions* to encourage a deeper understanding of the subject within students.
- *Provide ongoing feedback* so that students can continually be building on their knowledge and understanding of a topic.

5. Promote transfer and generalisability

- As time permits, *expose students to multiple examples* so that they learn to generalize concepts and skills across different contexts and applications.

- *Relate course material to the real world* and show how what students are learning affects their everyday lives and make links to the types of careers you expect them to pursue.

Summary of main points

- Encourage students to develop *intrinsic motivators* – an intrinsic interest in one area of the curriculum that students can use as knowledge anchors to which they can relate other course information.
- Intrinsic motivators can guide and motivate future inquiry.
- Mini-lectures should be restricted to approximately 15 minutes because students find it difficult to concentrate in a classroom when teachers talk for more than 20 minutes.
- Links between the various subject specifications need to be made clear so that students see that the examination specifications are not a mass of unrelated facts/information but are actually part of a coherent whole subject.
- Constructivist or PBL learning tasks are effective mechanisms for developing higher-order subject knowledge and understanding.
- Students need to use subject information to construct their own meaning and understanding of a topic.

10 Encouraging deep learning through coursework

The only source of knowledge is experience.

Albert Einstein

Traditionally, one of the central problems with coursework is that it is often introduced as a separate module distinct from the examination-based modules. This causes students to differentiate the theoretical aspects of the course from the practical. In coursework classes, students are guided through a series of exercises that teach them the practical subject-specific skills they will need to complete the coursework project. However, students will only learn subject-specific skills if they have the opportunity to apply those skills. For this reason, teachers need to create contexts that encourage students to use and apply these subject-specific skills while also making the links between theory and practice clear. Further, the context needs to simulate the real world. Students need to know that the skills they are learning have purpose and use in their lives and future careers.

Another difficulty with coursework is that students find it difficult to start a project and take responsibility for its direction because they do not know what the end product of such a project looks like. Therefore, teachers need to design a coursework class that over the year allows students to work through smaller, less intense projects that simulate the coursework process and gradually grow in complexity and demand a more complex skill set to be employed by the student as the term progresses. The key to teaching coursework modules effectively is not focusing on the learning of the subject-specific skills students will need to complete the project, but giving them the experience of the coursework process and understanding of the assessment criteria.

The model of 'interaction for instruction' introduced in Chapter 6 is a useful approach that can be applied to coursework teaching in the classroom. The key to coursework teaching is the gradual scaffolding process whereby the teacher relinquishes control of the learning environment to the student. The following are suggestions, presented chronologically, for teaching the coursework process.

Teaching domain and subject-specific skills

Students are guided through a series of exercises, often taught in isolation, that teach them the practical skills they need to complete their coursework. However, they find it difficult to then use those skills to complete the assignment because they cannot transfer those learned skills to the new context (i.e. the coursework project). Coursework teaching often puts too much focus on the basic subject-specific skills and it fails to deal with the application of those skills in a more complex way (e.g. applying multiple skills in a novel environment).

For example, an IT teacher teaching students how to use a spreadsheet will lead students through spreadsheet exercises or have the students complete textbook exercises on how to format text, resize and merge cells, insert formulas, create macros and generate graphs. These are all basic skills that students need to complete a spreadsheet coursework project. However, when the students are asked to design a spreadsheet that would record student grades, calculate percentages, hold multiple class lists and contain macros for generating graphs of the information, they fail to see how those basic techniques and skills can be combined in a more complex way. When the skills are taught over the course of a year in isolation as individual skills students have no conception of how these basic skills combine into a more complex skill set that can be applied in new and novel contexts (i.e. their eventual coursework project).

Every subject has skills in which students need to be competent. Teachers should start a coursework module by teaching the subject-specific skills needed in the context of a developing coursework example project. The same skills/techniques should be taught simultaneously in isolation using different examples and contexts. This allows students to compare how these skills are used and applied to their coursework and see that these skills are distinct techniques that can be applied to multiple contexts.

Applying subject-specific skills and developing a more complex skill set

Early on in the coursework module, when students have learned a repertoire of subject-specific skills, they should be encouraged to use those skills to construct or create something. This encourages students to construct their own knowledge and understanding by using the skills and developing the basic skills into a more complex skill set. While they may not yet have mastered all the skills needed to complete a coursework project, they will have learned enough to work on small projects/ assignments whereby they develop a more complex repertoire of skills in the process.

During these tasks students will encounter problems that cannot be solved using their current skill set and so they will attempt to use and adapt their current skill set to solve the problem. As they develop new skills, they will have 'Eureka' moments in which they learn new skills to solve a problem they have encountered in a more effective way. It is these moments when they resolve earlier instances of cognitive conflict that impact on their learning most directly. Further, this new understanding of the application of their skills will enhance their learning while their developing skill set continues to expand and become more complex.

Relinquishing control of the learning environment

There should be a gradual move from a teacher to student-directed learning environment. You will notice that I used the term 'directed' rather than 'centred'. This means that all learning activities will be student-centred but, during the initial classes, the teacher will direct which activities are to be completed. Gradually, this control is given to the students to engage in self-directed learning. In this context, self-directed learning can be achieved by assigning students small, single or double-lesson, individual or group projects that will allow them to apply their skills and knowledge to a simulated coursework project. When they come across skills or knowledge they may lack, it is their responsibility to seek the assistance of their peers, teacher or learning resources (e.g. textbooks, the Internet).

The key aspect of this process is that the small projects/ learning tasks grow in complexity, so that the last project they complete incorporates all the subject-based skills they need to complete their coursework. A useful technique is to write project tasks that allow the students to re-use what they have designed/constructed/built in the previous project. The important element is that the new task grows in complexity and demand. Over the course of a term, the students will have gone through a development process many times and can visualize what an end product for their coursework will look like when it has been completed.

Textbooks versus teacher–led learning

One of the most difficult aspects of coursework teaching is having enough time during the academic year for students to develop the subject-specific skills needed to complete the coursework. To teach these skills, many teachers may rely on textbook exercises. Textbooks are often written in a format that introduces knowledge and skills in an ascending order and are explicitly written based on examination board subject specifi-cations. The problem with having students use a textbook to learn the subject skills initially is that they are extremely time-consuming because they are dependent on the individual abilities of the student to read and complete the exercises. In addition, students often read through the exercises and follow the task directions with little or no reflection on what it is they are actually doing. Therefore, during the initial learning ses-sions, teachers may find it useful to use a model of instruction similar to the 'interaction for instruction' (introduced in Chapter 6). A simple model would follow the following format:

1. Teacher demonstrates knowledge/skill (K/S) while student observes.
2. Teacher demonstrates K/S while student simultaneously carries out task (multiple times depending on the complexity of the K/S).
3. Students demonstrate the K/S independently.
4. Students then extrapolate and use the K/S past the level expected in the current task.

This scaffolding process gradually relinquishes control of the learning process to the students and in the final phases encourages them to apply the K/S to a novel context. When students begin to do small, single or double-lesson individual or group project work, textbooks can be useful as a reference. Further, when students have learned the K/S, they can carry out textbook exercises more quickly because they do not have to follow word for word through the textbook. This can drastically reduce the amount of class time taken for textbook exercises.

Collaborative learning

Collaborative learning during coursework lessons is an extremely useful tool for teachers. Students often find learning from each other easier than learning from the teacher. Students in coursework classes should always be encouraged to ask for assistance from, and give assistance to, their peers. By teaching someone else, students must engage with the information from different perspectives and at a deeper level. This also reduces the demands made on the teacher in a class format that has traditionally been one where teachers run from student to student providing support. Further, if students are directed to assist other students with learning tasks, they gain a sense of pride and are encouraged to take more responsibility for their learning. Because students can assist each other with simpler problems, teachers can focus on the wider and more complex issues that arise from multiple students and deal with them centrally from the front of the class.

Another aspect of collaborative learning that works well in coursework classes is small group work. When students complete small projects together that are designed to simulate their coursework it allows them to see how their peers approach this work. It gives them the opportunity to view the learning tasks from different perspectives (i.e. through the eyes of their peers) and observe the problem-solving and critical thinking processes of their peers. This allows them to develop a more comprehensive and well-rounded approach to their coursework.

Student ownership of their learning – presenting their work

The final aspect of the coursework learning process is allowing students to demonstrate and present the work that they have completed. This includes both the individual and group work simulated projects and their formal coursework. Presenting their work to their peers encourages students to take pride in their work and responsibility for their learning. Knowing that other students will see their coursework gives students the motivation to exert a greater effort and work towards achieving a higher grade. During the year, when students complete the small coursework simulations, they can be given the opportunity to show their work to the rest of the class. This can be done via posters posted on the classroom walls, demonstrations at the front of the class or through a webpage. If students are presenting in a group, it is important that each student is given the opportunity to present an element of the completed work.

This process is also important through the year at the completion of each of their simulated coursework projects. Such a process allows students to experience how their peers have viewed the learning task, the way they have approached it and used the various subject-based skills in novel ways to complete the same project. This is important, because it allows students to see that there are multiple ways of approaching a task. Observing how someone else has completed the task gives them a broader understanding of the task and a deep understanding of their own learning processes.

Summary of main points

- One of the central problems with coursework is that it is often introduced as a separate module distinct from the examination-based modules.
- Students will only learn subject-specific skills if they have been given the opportunity to apply those skills.
- Teachers need to create contexts that encourage students to use and apply subject-specific skills while making the links between theory and practice clear.
- The learning tasks need to simulate the real world so that students understand that what they are learning has purpose and affects their lives.
- Students find it difficult to start a coursework project and take responsibility for its direction because they cannot visualize what the end product will look like.
- Teachers need to design a coursework class that, over the year, allows students to work through smaller, less intense projects that simulate the coursework process and gradually grow in complexity.
- The key to teaching coursework modules effectively is not focusing on students learning the needed skills but giving them the experience of the coursework process and understanding the assessment criteria.
- Coursework teaching often puts too much emphasis on the basic subject-specific skills and fails to deal with the application of those skills in more complex ways.
- Early on in the coursework module, when students have learned a repertoire of subject-specific skills, they should be encouraged to use those skills to construct or create something. This encourages students to construct their own knowledge and understanding by using the skills and combining the basic skills into a more complex skill set.
- As students develop new skills they will have 'Eureka' moments in which they learn new skills to solve a problem they have encountered in a more effective way.

- During coursework teaching there should be a gradual move from a teacher to student-directed learning environment.
- The problem with learning subject-based skills from a textbook is that students often read through the exercises and follow the task directions will little or no reflection on what it is they are actually doing.
- Students in coursework classes should always be encouraged to ask for assistance from, and give assistance to, their peers.

11 Feedback that encourages deep learning

The only thing that interferes with my learning is my education.
Albert Einstein

A significant component of contemporary schooling in FE is the summative assessment regimes that occur at the end of the academic year. The final examination is often a central focus throughout an academic year in many FE classrooms and the cause of great distress during the lead-up to examinations. The research indicates that the method of assessment is a major influence on how a student approaches their learning and studying (Entwistle *et al.* 2002). However, what does it mean when our students perform well in their examinations? What does it actually tell us? In some cases, it tells us that our students are spending more time in test preparation and that as teachers we are competent at preparing students for examinations, often done effectively by teaching-to-the-test. I have found (Weyers 2005) that when teachers felt under pressure to cover an extensive curriculum and meet achievement targets set by the government and their institutions, they often adopted strategies of teaching-to-the-test because it was the most effective way of getting their students through their examinations.

However, if our students perform well during an examination it does not tell us much about what our students are capable of, what they understand and what they are able to do. Most students and teachers in FE have become very adept at the assessment game. Final examinations from previous years are always available on examination board websites. When it comes time to review a topic, it is common for a teacher to pull questions from past papers and work through the answers with the students. Additionally, during examination time students and teachers pour over past papers attempting to deduce the types of questions that will be asked in the current year's examination. This is, of course, a completely valid way to prepare students to do well in their examinations in the current system. However, what we often forget is that there is much more to assessment than end-of-year summative examinations.

Feedback through marking

Butler (1988) investigated the effects that different types of feedback (grade, comments or a combination of grade and comments) had on three groups of learners. The study showed that learning gains were the greatest for the group given only comments with no effect for the other two groups (i.e. grade and combination). The study concluded that:

- students' first reaction when their work is graded is to compare their grade with that of their peers rather than read the comments;
- comments are often brief (e.g. 'good') and do not provide specific and constructive feedback;
- students are rarely given adequate time in class to read comments;
- students rarely acknowledge written comments on their work and continue to make the same mistakes.

Butler also found that students preferred teachers not to use red pen because it ruined their work and they wanted teachers to write clearly and legibly so that the comments could be read and understood. Too often in the classroom, we think of the work that we assign students as indicators of their progression in the course. We give them weekly homework assignments, they hand the assignment in and we give it a grade out of 10, 20, etc. We return the assignment with a few general comments like 'you need to explain this more clearly', 'keep up the good work' or 'you need to put more effort into your work'. We record the students' grades in our homework book so that we have suitable evidence of achievement and progression to show parents, the head of department or the college administration.

Teachers often adopt this assessment strategy because they are under tight time constraints and have extensive work demands. Students and teachers know that homework grades do not contribute to a student's final grade in most academic and vocational FE courses, so there is little motivation for students to put the level of detail and time into their work that would benefit their learning. Further, it is often clear to teachers when students have made partial attempts to complete assigned work and this discourages teachers from putting quality time into feedback on work that many students may have completed a few minutes before they came to class.

However, the difficulty is that students will not know how to improve their performance if they are not given proper feedback and suggestions for improvement. Black et al. (2003) found that to improve student performance through written feedback teachers need to provide:

- tasks that encourage students to develop and demonstrate their understanding of what they have learnt;
- comments that identify what has been done well, what still needs improvement and give guidance on how to accomplish it;
- opportunities in class to make the needed improvements with support from the teacher.

Assessing students' work and assigning them a grade may indicate what level they are currently working at; however, it does not indicate how to move to a higher level of performance. Thus, teachers need to give explicit feedback to students on what they need to do to improve (e.g. if the question asks you to . . . you need to give four points that indicate . . . and provide a justification for those points).

Peer and self-assessment

Peer and self-assessment can be valuable tools for helping students develop the skills needed to understand what is required of them and set targets to meet their learning goals. Using these forms of assessment with students helps make the learning outcomes clearer to the students. For example, when students are given the opportunity to grade their peers' answers on a homework assignment or mock examination they begin to assess their peers' answers against the assessment criteria and develop a more objective way of looking at their assessment. This gives them the opportunity to reflect back on the answers that they have written and consciously re-evaluate their own work.

Black *et al.* (2003) point out that peer assessment allows students to communicate using a language that they both understand. In addition, students will often take criticisms of their work from peers more seriously than comments made by their teachers. Similarly, teachers are able to use concrete examples from other students to demonstrate an acceptable and unacceptable standard of student work. Black *et al.* suggested:

- the evaluation criteria need to be clear to students so that they understand the standard of work that is expected of them. This can be done by using examples of successful student work;
- students should be encouraged to collaborate during peer assessment activities because it gives them the opportunity to develop the objectivity required for effective self-assessment;
- students should be encouraged to compare their own work against the assessment criteria.

When students are given the opportunity to see how their fellow peers have carried out a task, it allows them to see the task from a different perspective. When peer assessment is followed up with self-assessment, students can use this developed objectivity to understand more clearly what is expected of them and to evaluate their own work. In addition, by seeing the different ways in which their peers have approached an assessment task, students are enabled to build a deeper and well-rounded understanding of the task itself.

Assessment and feedback in coursework modules

An assessment and feedback process for coursework classes is outlined below:

1. *Simulated coursework projects* – After students have learned the basic subject skills, they should use those skills to construct a project similar to their eventual coursework. They should write introductory paragraphs describing their project and conclusions based on the project results. It should be assessed on the examination board assessment criteria. However, the assessment does not necessarily need to be completed by the teacher and can be completed by their peers or individually with supervision by the teacher. This allows students to start developing their understanding of the assessment criteria. The project and assessment should be handed in so that the teacher can keep track of student progress.

2. *Verbal feedback from the teacher* – An important element of feedback is the constant verbal feedback given by the teacher as students work on their projects. This is done most effectively by using effective questioning to query students and challenge them to think more critically about what it is they are doing (see Chapter 5). Further, teachers can verbalize their thinking processes out loud to students as they look at their project. This allows teachers to model higher-level thinking and encourages students to do the same. In addition, this verbal feedback process is a quicker way of keeping on top of student progress and giving students instant feedback rather than having them physically hand in their coursework through a series of stages.

3. *Peer assessment* – This peer-assessment process is the point at which students display their work to their peers. Following the initial completion of the coursework project students should be given time to assess their fellow peers' projects against the assessment criteria and provide written feedback. This can be done by having students move around the class changing their seats every

five to ten minutes, reading through their peers' projects and providing comments on a sheet of paper that is left with the project. When the students return to their project, they will have a list of suggestions that they can use to improve it.

4. *Self-assessment* – After students have made improvements to their coursework based on peer comments, they should be given the opportunity to evaluate their coursework in depth based on the examination board assessment criteria and to provide detailed notes/comments that they submit to the teacher. They will have had the opportunity to go through the assessment process already during the peer assessment exercise so will be familiar with some of the assessment criteria. The self assessment allows them to gauge how well they think their project meets the assessment criteria and allows the teacher to assess how closely aligned the student's understanding of the assessment criteria is to their own. This process can be used for an initial hand-in period where the teacher looks at the student's self-assessment and meets with them or provides written feedback to improve the project before a final deadline. (Please note: the idea of an initial hand-in date and a final hand-in date is a controversial topic and some teachers would argue that having an initial hand-in date could sometimes cause students to procrastinate because they know the deadline can always be extended.)

Summary of main points

- Students' first reaction when their work is graded is to compare their grade with that of their peers rather than read the comments.
- Comments are often brief (e.g. 'good') and do not provide specific and constructive feedback.
- Students are rarely given adequate time in class to read comments.
- Students rarely acknowledge written comments on their work and continue to make the same mistakes.

- Students prefer teachers not to use red pen because it ruins their work.
- Students prefer teachers to write clearly and legibly so that the comments can be read and understood.
- Students prefer teachers to set them tasks that encourage them to develop and demonstrate their understanding of what they have learnt.
- Comments should identify what has been done well, what still needs improvement and give guidance on how to accomplish it.
- Opportunities should be available in class to make the needed improvements with support from the teacher.
- The evaluation criteria need to be made explicit and clear to students so that they understand what it means to complete the work successfully.
- Students should be encouraged to collaborate during peer-assessment activities because it gives them the opportunity to develop the objectivity required for effective self-assessment.
- Students should be encouraged to continually assess their own work against the assessment criteria.

12 Conclusion

Teaching to encourage deep learning

This book and much of the research I have done to date has developed from the unease that I felt teaching in the FE sector. This concern was echoed in the Tomlinson Report (Tomlinson 2004a), written by the Working Group on 14–19 Reform, set up in Spring 2003 to address issues of low post-16 participation and achievement, and an over-burdensome curriculum and assessment system. The report argued that there were too many qualifications and that the mix of coursework and formal assessment means that students have too many external exams.

Meeting examination board specifications seems to take precedence over developing understanding in the FE classroom and can often act as a ceiling which limits the level of understanding expected of students. Under the pressures of a high workload, teachers tend to keep student-centred activities to a minimum and focus on knowledge transmission (didactic lecture-style methods) at the expense of student understanding. However, when teachers' workloads are manageable and they focus on encouraging understanding in the classroom, students tend to use deep approaches to studying.

In contrast, to deal with the substantive amount of subject information at the end of the academic year, students tend to adopt surface approaches (rote memorization) to studying and subsequently course satisfaction and final examination grades tend to be lower. We should teach and assess students in a way that encourages students to adopt a deep approach. Deep approaches to learning and studying are related to what students perceive as good teaching, while a heavy workload is linked to a surface approach.

As teachers, to encourage students to take a deep approach to their learning and studying, we need to show personal interest in the subject we are teaching. We need to bring out the structure of the subject and to concentrate on ensuring plenty of time for key concepts. We need to show our students the links that exist between the various topics in the course and the links between the separate course modules and units. Teachers need to be aware of the unconscious messages that they may inadvertently convey to students in a classroom, as these messages can affect the way that students approach their studies.

We need to encourage our students to be critical of accepted theories and views, which will encourage them to develop an awareness of the limited and provisional nature of current knowledge in all fields. We need to show students how understanding evolves and is subject to challenge and revision. Finally, we need to allow students to become active participants in the learning process by encouraging them to take part in discussions of the ways in which their study tasks can be undertaken.

Lesson design to encourage deep learning

During a lesson, mini-lectures should be restricted to approximately 15 minutes because students find it difficult to concentrate in a classroom when teachers talk for more than 20 minutes. Links between the various subject specifications need to be made clear so that students see the examination specifications not as a mass of unrelated facts and information, but as part of a coherent subject.

To encourage students to take a deep approach to their learning needs, a curriculum that presents the subject from multiple perspectives. As teachers, we need to act as a guide and facilitator rather than the expert. The learning environment, the activities and assessment should encourage problem solving, critical thinking and reflection. Our students need to take ownership of the learning process, and learning tasks need to be context-based and represent the complexities of the 'real world'. Knowledge construction and the development of higher-order thinking skills, rather than rote memorization and reproduction, should be emphasized in the classroom, learning activities and assessment. We should be encouraging students to seek knowledge independently and collaboratively.

Our students need to demonstrate critical thinking by applying their course information to real-world situations. PBL provides a powerful way to enhance learning in the classroom by involving students in motivating and challenging problems that prompt reflection and deep approaches to learning. PBL places students in real-world scenarios, which shows students how what they are learning affects their everyday lives. PBL uses learning activities that encourage the development of understanding and assesses learning in ways that demonstrate understanding. PBL develops students' collaboration, communication and problem-solving skills and promotes higher-order thinking by encouraging students to be critical, reflective and creative thinkers.

Coursework that encourages deep learning

One of the central problems with coursework is that it is often introduced as a separate module distinct from the examination-based theory modules. As teachers, we need to create contexts that encourage students to use and apply subject-specific skills which will make the links between theory and practice clearer. Coursework needs to simulate the discipline in the real world so that students can see that what they are learning has purpose and affects their lives. Students find it difficult to start a coursework project and take responsibility for its direction because they cannot visualize what the end product will look like. Therefore, we need to design our coursework classes in a way that will allow students to work through smaller, less intense projects that gradually grow in complexity over the course of the academic year.

The key to teaching coursework modules is not only emphasizing the subject skills students need but also giving them the experience of working through the coursework process and assisting them in understanding the assessment criteria. Coursework teaching often puts too much emphasis on the basic subject-specific skills in isolation and it fails to demonstrate the application of those skills to the project assignment. Early on in the coursework module, when students have learned a repertoire of subject-specific skills, we need to design exercises that encourage students to use the new skills to construct or create something that simulates their coursework project. This encourages students to construct their own knowledge and understanding by combining the basis skills into a more complex skill set.

As students develop a more complex skill set, they will have 'Eureka' moments in which they learn new skills to solve old problems in a more effective way. The difficulty with learning subject-based skills from a textbook is that students often read the exercises and follow the task directions with little or no reflection on what it is they are actually doing. During coursework teaching there should be a gradual move from a teacher to student-directed learning environment. In addition, students should always be encouraged to ask for, and provide, assistance from their peers as they reflect on what they are learning.

Things that discourage deep learning

Despite our best attempts, sometimes we unwittingly do things that discourage learning in the classroom. Avoid giving a lecture and talking too much in the classroom; rather, conduct a dialogue with your students. When you answer questions too quickly in class, you do not allow students to engage with the question. Further, when you do not immediately get the response you are looking for and you answer your own questions, it deprives students of the opportunity to construct and express their thoughts on the topic. Also, a rapid reward to a response favours students who are fast thinkers and may actually be biased against students who think more deeply and have longer processing times.

Do not allow a single student to dominate a discussion. In addition, avoid simply giving students answers, although it may seem easier at the time and it may be what the students seem to want, it is not what is best for their learning. Rather, have the class discuss possible solutions and possibilities. Do not allow students to simply respond to you; rather, create an atmosphere where students take part in discussions with each other and respond to questions by directing their answers to the entire class. When leading class discussions, prepare a mix of questions (easily answered, mildly challenging, highly complex) and use probing questions to facilitate inquiry and critical thinking. A good question is one that challenges student understanding and requires analysis, synthesis, interpretation and critical thinking in order to answer it. Your role in this learning process is to maintain a dialogue with the learner and to assist him/her in refining their understanding.

Conclusion

The majority of the research that underpins this book falls within the realm of what has come to be called *student learning research* (Biggs 1999). I have made some practical suggestions, derived from my experience of FE teaching, for teachers trying to meet the institutional demands of a standardized curriculum and examination system. I have attempted to present the research in an easily accessible way that leaves educators with the flexibility to personalize their own innovations and adapt these concepts and ideas to their own classrooms and institutions. As teachers, we have neither the time nor the energy to continually reinvent innovative classrooms. I hope this book has provided some practical suggestions, based on sound pedagogical principles and strategies, which will support teachers in transforming teaching and learning in their classrooms.

References

Atherton, J. S. (2005a) 'Learning and teaching: conversational learning theory – Systems and Conversations: Pask and Laurillard', www.learningandteaching.info/learning/pask.htm#Conversational. Last accessed: 17 November 2005.

Atherton, J. S. (2005b) 'Learning and teaching: deep and surface learning', www.learningandteaching.info/learning/deepsurf.htm. Last accessed: 24 November 2005.

Atherton, J. S. (2005c) 'Learning and Teaching: SOLO taxonomy', www.learningandteaching.info/learning/solo.htm: Last accessed: 15 November 2005.

Balla, J. I., Biggs, J. B., Gibson, M. and Chang, A. M. (1990) 'The application of basic science concepts to clinical problem-solving' in *Medical Education*, 24, 137–47.

Barrows, H. S. (2000), 'Foreword' in Evenson, D. and Hmelo, C. (eds) *Problem-based Learning: A Research Perspective on Learning Interactions*. Mahwah, NJ: Lawrence Erlbaum Associates, ppvii-ix.

Barrows, H. S. (2003) *Generic Problem-based Learning Essentials*, www.pbli.org/pbl/generic_pbl.htm. Last accessed: 12 March 2003.

Beaty, E., Gibbs, G. and Morgan, A. (1997) 'Learning orientations and study contracts' in Marton, F., Hounsell D. J. and Entwistle N. J. (eds) *The Experience of Learning* (2nd edn). Edinburgh: Scottish Academic Press, pp. 72–88

Berryman, S. (1991) 'Designing effective learning environments: Cognitive apprenticeship models' in *IEE-Brief*, 1 September 1991.

Biggs, J. B. (1987) *Student Approaches to Learning and Studying*. Melbourne: Australian Council for Educational Research.

Biggs, J. B. (1989) 'Approaches to the enhancement of tertiary teaching', in *Higher Education Research and Development*, 8, 7–25.

Biggs, J. B. (1996) 'Enhancing teaching through constructive alignment' in *Higher Education*, 32, 1–18.

Biggs, J. B. (1999) *Teaching for Quality Learning*, 1st edn. Buckingham: Society for Research into Higher Education and Open University Press.

Biggs, J. B. (2003) *Teaching for Quality Learning*, 3rd edn. Buckingham: Society for Research into Higher Education and Open University Press.

Biggs, J. B. and Collis, K. (1982) *Evaluating the Quality of Learning: the SOLO Taxonomy*. New York: Academic Press.

Black, P., Harrison, C., Lee, C., Marshall, B. and Wiliam, D. (2003) *Assessment for Learning: Putting it into Practice*. London: Open University Press.

Bloom, B., Englehart, M., Furst, E., Hill, W. and Krathwohl, D. (1956) *Taxonomy of Educational Objectives: The Classification of Educational Goals. Handbook I: Cognitive Domain*. New York: Longmans Green.

Boud, D. and Feletti, G. (1997) *The Challenge of Problem-based Learning* (2nd edn). London: Kogan Page.

Bruner, J. S. (1966) *Toward a Theory of Instruction*. Cambridge, MA: Belkapp Press.

Butler, R. (1988) 'Enhancing and undermining intrinsic motivation: the effects of task-involving and ego-involving evaluation on interest and performance' in *British Journal of Educational Psychology*, 58, 1–14.

Calderhead, J. (1996) 'Teachers: beliefs and knowledge' in Berliner, D.C. and Calfee, R.C. (eds) *Handbook of Educational Psychology*. New York: Macmillan.

Carr, K. (1990) 'How can we teach critical thinking?' in *ERIC Digest* (Eric no.: ED326304). http://chiron.valdosta.edu/whuitt/files/critthnk.html. Last accessed: October 2005.

Carroll, J. (1963) 'A model of school learning' in *Teachers College Record*, 64, 723–33.

Coffield, F., Moseley, D., Hall, E. and Ecclestone, K. (2004) 'Should we be using learning styles? What research has to say to practice'. Learning and Skills Research Centre, www.lsda.org.uk/pubs/dbase out/download.asp?code=1540. Last accessed: 20 November 2005.

Cognition and Technology Group at Vanderbilt (CTGV) (1991) 'Technology and the design of generative learning environments' in *Educational Technology*, May, 34–40.

'Constructivism and instructivism' (n.d.), www.worc.ac.uk/LTMain/LTC/StaffDev/Constructivism/. Last accessed: 15 October 2005.

De Grave, W., Schmidt, H. and Boshuisen, H. (2001) 'Effects of problem-based discussion on studying a subsequent test: A randomised trial among first year medical students' in *Instructional Science*, 29, 33–44.

DfES (2002a) *Success For All: Reforming Further Education and Training*. London: DfES.

DfES (2002b) *14–19: Extending Opportunities, Raising Standards*. London: DfES.

Diaz, D. P. and Bontenbal, K. F. (2000) 'Pedagogy-based technology training', in Hoffman, P. and Lemke D. (eds) *Teaching and Learning in a Network World*. Amsterdam: IOS Press, pp. 50–4.

Dolmans, D. and Schmidt, H. (2000) 'What directs self-directed learning in a problem-based curriculum?' in Evenson, D. and Hmelo, C. (eds) *Problem-based Learning: A Research Perspective on Learning Interactions*. Mahwah, NJ: Lawrence Erlbaum Associates, pp. 251–62.

Drew, P. Y. and Watkins, D. (1998) 'Affective variables, learning approaches and academic achievement: a causal modelling investigation with Hong Kong tertiary students' in *British Journal of Educational Psychology*, 68, 173–88.

Duckworth, E. (1987) '*The Having of Wonderful Ideas' and other Essays on Teaching and Learning*. New York: Teachers College Press.

Duemler, D. and Mayer, R. (1988) 'Hidden costs of reflectiveness: Aspects of successful scientific reasoning' in *Journal of Educational Psychology*, 80 (4), 419–23.

Eley, M. G. (1992) 'Differential adoption of study approaches within individual students' in *Higher Education*, 23, 231–54.

Elwood, J. (1999) 'Gender, achievement and the "Gold Standard": differential performance in the GCE A level examination' in *Curriculum Journal*, 10 (2), 189–208.

Engineering Subject Centre – Higher Education Academy, www.engsc. ac.uk/er/theory/learning.asp. Last accessed: 1 November 2005.

Enhancing Education @ Carnegie Mellon (2002), www.cmu.edu/ teaching/resources/index.html. Last accessed: 1 December 2005.

Entwistle, N. J. (1998a) 'Approaches to learning and forms of understanding' in Dart B. and Boulton-Lewis, G. (eds) *Teaching and Learning in Higher Education*. Melbourne: Australian Council for Educational Research.

Entwistle, N. J. (1998b) 'Improving teaching through research on student learning' in Forest, J. J. F. (ed.) *University Teaching: International Perspectives*. New York: Garland.

Entwistle, N. J. (1994) 'Generative concepts and pedagogical fertility: communicating research findings on student learning' in *EARLI News*, June 1994, 9–15.

Entwistle, N., McCune, V. and Hounsell, J. (2002) 'Approaches to studying and perceptions of university teaching-learning environments: concepts, measures and preliminary findings' in *Occasional Report 1: Teaching and Learning Research Program*. Edinburgh: University of Edinburgh.

Entwistle, N. J. and Ramsden, P. (1983) *Understanding Student Learning*. London: Croom Helm.

Entwistle, N. J. and Smith, C. A. (2002) 'Personal understanding and target understanding: mapping influences on the outcomes of learning' in *British Journal of Educational Psychology*, 72, 321–4.

Evenson, D. and Hmelo, C. (eds) (2000) *Problem-based Learning: A Research Perspective on Learning Interactions*. London: Lawrence Erlbaum Associates.

Finn, C. E. and Ravitch, D. (1996) 'Education Reform: A report from the educational excellence network to its education policy committee and the American people', www.edexcellence.net/library/epciv.html. Last accessed: 25 September 2002.

Fransson, A. (1977) 'On qualitative differences in learning. IV – Effects of motivation and test anxiety on process and outcome' in *British Journal of Educational Psychology*, 47, 244–57.

Frederick, P. (1981) 'The dreaded discussion: ten ways to start' in *Improving College and University Teaching*, 29 (3), 109–14.

Gagné, R. (1965) *The Conditions of Learning and the Theory of Instruction* (4th edn). New York: Holt, Rinehart and Winston.

Gardiner, L. F. (1998) 'Why we must change: the research evidence' in *The NEA Higher Education Journal*, Spring 1998, 71–88.

Ginnis, P. (2002) *The Teacher's Toolkit: Raise Classroom Achievement with Strategies for Every Learner*. Wales: Crown House Publishing.

Good, T. L. and Brophy, J. E. (1991) *Looking in Classrooms* (5th edn). New York: HarperCollins.

Harlen, W. and Deakin Crick, R. (2002) 'A systematic review of the impact of summative assessment and tests on students' motivation for learning' (EPPI-Centre Review), in *Research Evidence in Education Library*, 1. London: EPPI-Centre, Social Science Research Unit, Institute of Education, University of London.

Huitt, W. (1996) 'Summary of principles of direct instruction' in *Educational Psychology Interactive*. Valdosta, GA: Valdosta State University, http://chiron.valdosta.edu/whuitt/col/instruct/dirprn.html. Last accessed: 5 October 2005.

Huitt, W. (1997) 'A transactional model of the teaching/learning process' in *Educational Psychology Interactive*. Valdosta, GA: Valdosta State University, http://chiron.valdosta.edu/whuitt/materials/sysmdlo.html. Last accessed: 05 October 2005.

Jennings, M. (1994) 'Comparative Analysis, HyperCard, and the Future of Social Studies Education'. Paper presented at the Annual Meetings of the National Council for the Social Studies. Phoenix, AZ: 18 November 1994.

Johanssen, D. (1994) 'Thinking technology' in *Educational Technology*, 34 (4), 34–7.

Kember, D. (1996) 'The intention to both memorise and understand: another approach to learning' in *Higher Education*, 31, 341–54.

Krathwol, D. and Anderson, L. (2000) *A Taxonomy of Learning for Teaching: A Revision of Bloom's Taxonomy of Educational Objectives*. New York: Addison-Wesley-Longman.

Kruse, K. (2005) '*Gagné's Nine Events of instruction: An introduction*', www.e-learningguru.com/articles/art3_3.htm. Last accessed: 28 November 2005.

Laurillard, D. (1993) *Rethinking University Teaching: A Framework for the Effective Use of Educational Technology*. London: RoutledgeFalmer.

Laurillard, D. (2002) *Rethinking University Teaching: A framework for the effective use of educational technology* (2nd edn). London: RoutledgeFalmer.

Lipman, M. (1991) *Thinking in Education*. Cambridge: Cambridge University Press.

Lizzio, A., Wilson, K. and Simons, R. (2002) 'University students' perceptions of the learning environment and academic outcomes: implications for theory and practice' in *Studies in Higher Education*, 2 (1), 27–52.

Lucas, S. (2002) 'AIL 601: principles of instructional technology', http://susanlucas.com/it/ail601/instructivism.html. Last accessed: 27 October 2005.

Lumby, J. (2003) 'Leadership for learning: the case of further education'. The inaugural lecture of Professor Jacky Lumby, presented at the University of Lincoln, 15 May 2003.

McCune, V. (2003) 'Promoting high-quality learning: perspectives from the ETL Project Norwegian Network in Higher Education' 14th Conference on University and College Pedagogy, Frederikstad, 22–3 October 2003.

Malibar, I. and Pountney, D. C. (2002) 'Using technology to integrate constructivism and visualisation in mathematics education'. Paper presented at the second International Conference on the Teaching of Mathematics, Hersonissos, Crete, Greece, 1–6 July 2002.

Margules, D. (1996) 'Instructivism or constructivism: which end of the continuum?' Paper given at the AUC Academic Conference 'From Virtual to Reality', University of Queensland.

Marsh, G. (n.d.) 'Instructivism', www.healthnet.org.np/training/software/WW190.htm. Last accessed: 20 October 2005.

Marsh, G. (n.d.) 'Problem-based learning', www.healthnet.org.np/training/software/WW195.htm. Last accessed: 5 October 2005.

Marton, F. and Booth, S. (1997) *Learning and Awareness*. Mahwah, NJ: Lawrence Erlbaum Associates.

Marton, F., Hounsell, D. J. and Entwistle, J. J. (eds) (1997) *The Experience of Learning* (2nd edn). Edinburgh: Scottish Academic Press.

Marton, F. and Säljö, R. (1976) 'Symposium: learning processes and strategies. On qualitative differences in learning II: Outcome as a function of the learner's conception of the task' in *British Journal of Educational Psychology*, 46, 115–27.

Marton, F. and Säljö, R. (1997) 'Approaches to learning' in Marton, F., Hounsell, D. J. and Entwistle, N. J. (eds) *The Experience of Learning* (2nd edn). Edinburgh: Scottish Academic Press.

Mason, L. and Boscolo, P. (2000) 'Writing and conceptual change. What changes?' in *Instructional Science*, 28, 199–226.

Meyer, J. H. F. (2000) 'Variation in contrasting forms of "memorising" and associated observables' in *British Journal of Educational Psychology*, 70, 163–76.

Murphy, E. (1997) 'Constructivism from Philosophy to Practice', www.cdli.ca/~murphy/emurphy/cle.html. Last accessed: 25 November 2005.

Noddings, N. (1993) 'Constructivism and caring' in Davis, R. and Maher, C. (eds) *Schools, Mathematics and the World of Reality*. Boston, MA: Allyn and Bacon.

Paul, R. (1993) *Critical Thinking: How to Prepare Students for a Rapidly Changing World*. Santa Rosa, CA: Foundation for Critical Thinking.

Paul, R. and Elder, L. (1997) 'Foundation For Critical Thinking', www.criticalthinking.org. Last accessed: 15 November 2005.

Perkins, D. (1991) 'Technology meets constructivism: do they make a marriage?' in *Educational Technology*, May, 18–23.

Prosser, M. and Millar, R. (1989) 'The "how" and "what" of learning physics' in *European Journal of Psychology of Education*, 4, 513–28.

Prosser, M. and Trigwell, K. (1999) *Understanding Learning and Teaching in Deep and Surface Learning*. UK: Society for Research into Higher Education and Open University Press.

Ramsden, P. (1992) *Learning to Teach in Higher Education*. London: Routledge.

Ramsden, P. (1997) 'The context of learning in academic departments' in Marton, F. Hounsell D. J., and Entwistle N. (eds) *The Experience of Learning* (2nd edn). Edinburgh: Scottish Academic Press, pp. 198–216.

Ramsden, P., Beswick, D. G. and Bowden, J. A. (1986) 'Effects of academic departments on students' approaches to studying' in *British Journal of Educational Psychology*, 51, 368–83.

Reid, W. A. (1987) 'Institutions and practices: professional education reports and the language of reform' in *Educational Researcher*, 16 (8), 10–15.

Ritzer, G. (2000) *The McDonaldization of Society: An Investigation into the Changing Character of Contemporary Social Life.* London: Sage Publications.

Rosenshine, B. and Stevens, R. (1986) 'Teaching functions' in Wittrock, M. C. (ed.) *Handbook of Research on Teaching* (3rd edn). New York: Macmillan.

Savery, J. R. and Duffy, T. M. (1995) 'Problem-based learning: an instructional model and its constructivist framework' in *Educational Technology*, 35 (5), 31–7.

Scardamalia, M. and Bereiter, C. (1987) 'Knowledge telling and knowledge transforming in written composition' in Rosenberg, S. (ed.), *Advances in Applied Psycholinguistics, Vol. 2 Reading, Writing and Language Learning.* Cambridge: Cambridge University Press.

Schmidt, H. and Moust, J. (2000) 'Factors affecting small group tutorial learning: a review of research' in Evenson, D. and Hmelo, C. (eds) *Problem-based Learning: A Research Perspective on Learning Interactions.* London: Lawrence Erlbaum Associates.

Scouller, K. (1998) 'The influence of assessment method on students' learning approaches: multiple choice question examination versus assignment essay', in *Higher Education*, 35, 453–2.

Seddon, G. (1978) 'The properties of Bloom's taxonomy of educational objectives for the cognitive domain' in *Review of Educational Research*, 48 (2), 303–23.

Shulman, L. S. (1987) 'Knowledge and teaching: foundations of the new reform' in *Harvard Education Review*, 57, 114–35.

Slavin, R. (1995) 'A model of effective instruction' *The Educational Forum, Winter*, 59, pp. 166–76.

Slavin, R. (1997) *Educational Psychology: Theory and Practice* (5th edn). Needham Heights, MA: Allyn and Bacon, pp. 310–13.

Slavin, R. (2006) *Educational Psychology* (8th edn). Boston: Pearson/Allyn and Bacon.

Smith, C. A. (1998) 'Personal understanding and target understanding: their relationships through individual variations and curricular influences'. Unpublished Ph.D. thesis, University of Edinburgh.

Stanford University, Centre for Teaching and Learning (2004) 'Designing effective discussion questions', http://ctl.stanford.edu/handouts/. Last accessed: 30 October 2005.

Stephenson, J. and Weil, S. (1992) *Quality in Learning: A Capability Approach to Higher Education.* London: Kogan Page.

Stepien (1999a) *Northern Illinois University Consortium for Problem-based Learning*, www-ed.fnal.gov/trc/tutorial/taxonomy.html. Last accessed: 30 October 2005.

Stepien (1999b) 'Tutorial on problem-based learning', Northern Illinois

University Consortium for Problem-based Learning, www-ed.fnal. gov/trc/tutorial/pbl.html#anchor487665. Last accessed: 30 October 2005.

Tang, C. (1991) 'Effects of Different Assessment Methods on Tertiary Students' Approaches to Studying', Unpublished Ph.D. thesis, University of Hong Kong.

Thomas, P. R. and Bain, J. D. (1984) 'Contextual dependence of learning approaches: the effects of assessment' in *Human Learning*, 3, 227–40.

Tomlinson, M. (2004a) 'Final Report of the Working Group on 14–19 reform', www.14–19reform.gov.uk. Last accessed: 18 May 2005.

Tomlinson, M. (2004b) 'Summary of the Final Report of the Working Group on 14–19 Reform', http://publications.teachernet.gov.uk/ eOrderingDownload/DfE–0976–2004.pdf. Last accessed: 18 May 2005.

Trigwell, K. R. and Prosser, M. (1991) 'Improving the quality of student learning: the influence of learning context and student approaches to learning on learning outcomes' in *Higher Education*, 22, 251–66.

Trigwell, K. R. and Sleet, R. J. (1990) 'Improving the relationship between assessment results and student understanding' in *Assessment and Evaluation in Higher Education*, 13, 290–97.

Van Rossum, E. J. and Schenk, S. M. (1984) 'The relationship between learning conception, study strategy and learning outcomes' in *British Journal of Educational Psychology*, 54, 73–83.

von Glasersfeld, E. (1995) *Radical Constructivism: A Way of Knowing and Learning*. Washington: Falmer.

Vygotsky, L. (1978) *Mind in Society: The Development of Higher Psychological Processes* MA: Harvard University Press.

Watkins, D. A. and Biggs, J. B. (eds) (1996) *The Chinese Learner: Cultural, Psychological and Contextual Influences*. Hong Kong: Comparative Education Research Centre and Australian Council for Educational Research.

Watts, M. and Bentley, D. (1987) 'Constructivism in the classroom: enabling conceptual change by words and deeds' in *British Educational Research Journal*, 13 (2), 121–35.

Weyers, M. (2005) 'The process – product metaphor of education and the effects of examination boards on teaching and learning: an analysis of the teaching-learning environment in advanced subsidiary education'. Unpublished Ed.D. thesis, IIEL, University of Lincoln.

Whelan, G. (1988) 'Improving medical students' clinical problem solving' in Ramsden, P. (ed.) *Improving Learning: New Perspectives*. London: Kogan Page.

Wiley, J. and Voss, J. (1999) 'Constructing arguments from multiple sources: tasks that promote understanding and not just memory for text' in *Journal of Educational Psychology*, 91 (2), 301–11.

Wilkinson, G., Murray-Harvey, R. and Handsley, E. (n.d.) 'Aims and learning outcomes', www.flinders.edu.au/teach/topic/aims.htm# top#top. Last accessed: 5 September 2005.

Wilson, B. and Cole, P. (1991) 'A review of cognitive teaching models' in *Educational Technology Research and Development*, 39 (4), 47–64.

Wittrock, M. (ed.) (1986) *Handbook of Research on Teaching* (3rd edn). New York: Macmillan.

Wolff, A. (2000) *Problem-based Learning. The Role of the Tutor: A Resource Guide for Faculty*. Vancouver: Wolff Consulting Ltd.

Index